When "No" Isn't An Option!
Turning Failure Into Success

Marcus Thigpen

But you are not like that, for you are a chosen people. You are royal priests, a holy nation, God's very own possession. As a result, you can show others the goodness of God, for he CALLED YOU out of the darkness into his wonderful light.

1 Peter 2:9

Copyright © 2024 Marcus Thigpen

All rights reserved. No part of this book may be used or reproduced by any means, graphic, electronic, or mechanical, including photocopying, recording, taping or by any information storage retrieval system without the written permission of the publisher except in the case of brief quotations embodied in critical articles and reviews.

Printed in the United States of America

ISBN:9 781733 432504

Table of Contents

Dedication vii

Acknowledgments viii

Introduction 1

Overtime 4

Pre-Game Ritual 5

The Prayer 7

Chapter 1: Unnecessary Roughness 9

Chapter 2: False Start 26

Chapter 3: First Down 40

Chapter 4: Unsportsmanlike Conduct 58

Chapter 5: Suspended 73

Chapter 6: Timeout 86

Chapter 7: Victory 95

Salvation Prayer 106

DEDICATION

This book is dedicated to the courageous souls who confront challenges head-on and triumph over obstacles. To those lionhearted individuals who've felt the sting of disappointment, the weight of doubt, yet never let others' perceptions define them. Your dreams are not just possible but worthy of every sacrifice you make to reach them. Keep pushing forward. You are capable! I have full faith in you and know you possess the strength needed to succeed.

To my cherished children, **Dime Dime, MJ, Riya, Momo, Rae, Lay**, and our soon-to-arrive princess, **Jada**! Know this always and hold it dear: your daddy's love for you knows no bounds. With determination, passion, and hard work, you can conquer any challenge. Keep Christ not only at the center but also at the genesis and culmination of all you do, and there will be no limits to what you can achieve. You are my motivation, and I am blessed to guide and care for you.

ACKNOWLEDGMENTS

This book owes its existence to the incredible individuals who have shaped my life. My deepest gratitude goes to:

Leah Albright-Byrd, my beautiful wife, my sanctuary of joy, my Covenant Mate, my tranquil harbor, my eternal love. Your unwavering support, your timely arrival in my life, and the light you ignited when darkness seemed overwhelming, are treasures beyond measure. Your ability to inspire and challenge me, urging me to aspire to greater heights simply by being near, fills me with boundless gratitude. My love for you knows no bounds.

Lance Bennett, my spiritual mentor and brother, you've been my steadfast guide since the day you introduced me to Christ. Your life embodies the pursuit of God's heart, setting a standard I aspire to reach. Thank you for your continual investment in me, for your selflessness and unwavering support. Your life is a testament to what it means to walk in God's purpose. I appreciate you more than words can express, my brother!

Pastor Mike Todd (Transformation Church), My pastor and mentor from a distance, your influence has been instrumental in shaping the spiritual man I am today over these past eight transformative years. Your obedience to your calling and your global ministry has impacted countless lives, mine included. From "Expect Effect" to "Overflow," your teachings have pushed me to confront challenges head-on, compelling me to introspect and cease evading issues, knowing that God can only heal what I am willing to reveal. Through your guidance, I have embraced continual growth and positive changes, becoming a better person in every aspect. I am deeply grateful for your wisdom and leadership!

Pastor Steven Furtick (Elevation Church), My distant mentor, your guidance has been a beacon of strength and inspiration for me. During the challenging days of the pandemic when I was living in my car and working tirelessly for Amazon, your words sustained me every morning. Even now, I continue to find solace and motivation in the short clips you share. In moments when I teetered on the edge of giving up and losing hope, it was your wisdom from the vault that anchored me. Thank you for being a constant source of encouragement and light in my life!

Nick Polk, My brother from another mother. A companion on this journey for the past 19 years, and I treasure our friendship deeply. Your spirit-led guidance ensures I stay on track, never allowing me to stray. You fearlessly challenged me, corrected me when needed, and breathed hope into me during my lowest moments. Your unwavering support played a pivotal role in keeping me steadfast. Thank you for standing by my side as we navigate life's twists and turns together. I hold you in high regard, my friend!!

INTRODUCTION

Have you ever found yourself in a sporting event where your team was dominating, seemingly on the brink of victory, only to witness a sudden turnaround by the opponent? Or perhaps you've eagerly watched your favorite team poised to clinch a championship, only to witness them stumble in the final moments? These experiences often trigger a flood of questions and emotions, causing us to scrutinize decisions or vocalize frustrations at the screen. Phrases like "What were they thinking?" or "Why that particular play?" or even "Take them out of the game!" or "Can't they see what's happening, I'm looking at the screen and can see that?" echo through our minds, mirroring our exasperation and disbelief. But what unfolds in these critical junctures? Teams or individual players who once appeared indomitable can unexpectedly lose their momentum, leaving spectators and participants alike bewildered. Reflecting on my encounters with such scenarios, numerous factors contribute to these pivotal shifts. Fatigue gradually sets in, sapping the energy reserves of even the most resilient athletes. Key players may sustain minor injuries that lingers, disrupting the team's rhythm and strategy. Concentration levels fluctuate, leading to missed opportunities and lapses in judgment. Opponents adeptly strategize, exploiting vulnerabilities and turning the tide in their favor. The presence of exceptional coaches and players on both teams transforms the game into a captivating clash of determination among the players and a strategic showdown among the coaches. This rivalry not only makes attending the match worthwhile but also entices viewers to spend three thrilling hours in front of their television screens. Moreover, a sense of complacency can insidiously creep in, causing individuals to underestimate the opposition's determination and resilience. Despite valiant efforts, the ebb and flow of momentum can pivot decisively, or the opposing team might simply possess superior skills and coordination, outmatching their counterparts.

Now, transpose this dynamic to organizational environments: envision a talented team brimming with potential, capable of effecting substantial positive change. Yet, internal factors such as dwindling motivation or external distractions cast a pall over their performance, leading to a cascading negative impact. Just as in sports, where each team member's commitment and contribution significantly influence overall outcomes, a single individual's lack of engagement can reverberate throughout the entire team, compromising collective efficacy. In the subsequent discourse, I aim to delve into strategies and insights crucial for maintaining equilibrium in life's multifaceted arenas. Recognizing and addressing unseen obstacles and challenges, no matter how seemingly insignificant at onset, prevents their accumulation and eventual debilitating effects. Consider these moments as opportunities to call a strategic timeout, take a step back, catch your breath, reassess your approach, and hydrate before getting back in the game.

OVERTIME

In the event of a tie at the conclusion of a game, a coin toss determines which team gains possession first. Each team then has a chance to score during an additional 10-minute quarter, aiming to secure victory. Overtime rules vary across different levels of play, such as high school or college football, but let's focus on the NFL overtime rules for this discussion. In NFL overtime, both teams receive an opportunity to possess the ball unless the team receiving the kickoff scores a touchdown on their initial possession. If the defense intercepts the ball and scores a touchdown, or recovers a fumble for a touchdown, or even records a safety, the game concludes immediately. This scenario occurs because the defense successfully halted the offense's drive and simultaneously scored points, effectively ending the game.

Understanding these rules can be intricate, so let's delve deeper if needed. Stay with me as we clarify any complexities.

PRE-GAME RITUAL

Crafting and adhering to pre-game rituals is a deeply personal journey for athletes, an art honed over time to serve unique and multifaceted purposes. These rituals transcend mere superstition, acting as anchors of mental fortitude, confidence boosters, and avenues for emotional and physical preparation under the unforgiving glare of the spotlight. In my case, my pre-game ritual evolved into a profound blend of spirituality and mental imagery, primarily centered around prayer and visualization. Before stepping onto the field, I would pause to offer thanks to Jesus Christ for the gifts bestowed upon me—the athletic prowess, the platform to inspire, and the opportunity to positively impact not just budding athletes but also my cherished family and the larger community that embraced me. Following this moment of gratitude and spiritual grounding, I would immerse myself in vivid mental scenarios, meticulously rehearsing each play, envisioning flawless execution similarly to our meticulously drilled practice sessions day in and day out. This mental imagery not only prepared my body for optimal performance but also strengthened my mind against doubts and anxieties. I grappled with the awareness that my performance was under scrutiny, and my future opportunities depended on my present performance, particularly in a career marked by transience. This phase of the game provided me with the necessary foundation, fostering a quiet yet steadfast confidence in both my personal abilities and the collective strength of our team. Upon completing the arduous journey of writing my first book, I shared a rather naive excerpt with my supporters—a rallying cry encapsulated in the words: "I don't know what my future holds, but I will be prepared to take on whatever life throws at me." Looking back now, those words echo with youthful optimism and zeal with minimal lived experience yet a testament to my unyielding spirit and determination to face life's challenges head-on, regardless of their magnitude or complexity. Just as in sports, where overtime heralds a fresh start despite past triumphs or setbacks, I approached life with the same resilience and readiness. The reset button was pressed, and the scoreboard set back to 0-0, symbolizing not an end but a new beginning—a chance to showcase resilience, adaptability, and unwavering determination in the face of adversity.

Here's the prayer I offered after that bold declaration, as we prepared to face our opponent in overtime.

THE PRAYER

Heavenly Father,

I come before you humbly, acknowledging the blessings You have bestowed upon me—a loving family, a comfortable home, and the privilege to pursue my passion in the NFL, a dream I've cherished and chased since childhood. Gratitude fills my heart for these abundant blessings, yet I feel a stirring within me, a desire to transcend personal success and impact lives on a broader scale. I yearn to connect with people on a deeper level, to understand their struggles, and offer genuine help and inspiration. I've been immersing myself in the stories of motivational speakers who have traversed challenging paths, their resilience and triumphs resonating deeply within me. Their ability to turn adversity into motivation fuels my own aspirations—to have a narrative that can ignite hope and drive positive change in the world. I want to have a story that resonates with people alike. Though I've endured trying times, I need to be more connected through lived experiences of my own. Father, I seek Your guidance and empowerment in this journey. I pray that you grant me the wisdom to craft a compelling story that touches hearts and minds, sparking motivation and resilience in those who hear it. I ask that you open doors for me to reach diverse audiences and platforms where my experiences can bring light to darkened paths and strength to weary souls. Partner with me, Lord, as a vessel of Your love and grace, that through my journey and testimony, others may find solace, inspiration, and renewed faith in their own paths. I surrender myself to Your Will, ready to be an instrument of Your peace and love in this world. I pray for continued protection and blessings over my family, friends, and all those whose lives intersect with mine. May Your guiding hand be ever present, leading us on paths of righteousness and purpose.

In the name of Jesus, I pray. Amen.

CHAPTER 1: UNNECESSARY ROUGHNESS

Forcibly hitting the defenseless player's head, neck, or face with the helmet or facemask, regardless of whether the defensive player also uses his arms to tackle the defenseless player by encircling or grasping him. Penalty: For unnecessary roughness: Loss of 15 yards. The player may be disqualified if the action is judged by the official(s) to be flagrant.

"Marcus, do you think there's a chance things could turn around for me? I'm at rock bottom financially, back living with my mom, and struggling to find stable work. Any advice or connections that could help me climb out of this hole? Honestly, I can't see a way out right now!"

One day, while unwinding in the sauna at the gym, I struck up a conversation with a familiar face I often saw during my workouts. As our chat deepened, he opened up about his current struggles—empty pockets, returning to live with family, and job instability. He looked to me for guidance or any lifelines that could offer a glimmer of hope in his bleak circumstances. His despair was palpable; he felt trapped with no clear path forward. What he didn't know was that just a few months earlier, I too had faced a similar storm. While I hadn't moved back in with my mom, I could empathize with the financial and emotional rollercoaster he was enduring. Ironically, during our conversation that day, I had just finished praying and crying as I was reflecting on my own journey. In that transformative month, my life seemed to burst with significant milestones, each marking a profound shift in my journey. It was a time of renewal, growth, and accomplishment that resonated deeply within me. One of the most pivotal moments was renewing my faith through water baptism. It signified not just a spiritual rebirth but also a commitment to a new way of living and understanding my purpose. This step brought a sense of clarity and peace that anchored me during the upcoming transitions. Securing my own apartment was a symbol of newfound independence and stability.

It marked a shift from previous uncertainties to a more structured and intentional living arrangement. The freedom to create my space, tailored to my needs and aspirations, was both empowering and liberating. Celebrating my 35th birthday took on a special significance against this backdrop of personal growth. It wasn't just about marking another year but acknowledging the progress, resilience, and lessons learned along the way. It was a moment of gratitude for the journey thus far and anticipation for the path ahead. The celebratory trip abroad that I took was a well-deserved reward—a moment to pause, reflect, and bask in the joy of achievements. Stepping into new cultural landscapes and experiences broadened my perspective and added layers of richness to my life story. Completing my master's degree, despite the challenges posed by the Covid-19 pandemic, represented perseverance and dedication. The online graduation, while different from traditional ceremonies, still held the same essence of accomplishment and pride. It was a testament to adapting to circumstances while staying focused on long-term goals.

Wrapping up my NFL internship was a culmination of insights gained, skills honed, and connections made. It provided a bridge between my athletic background and professional aspirations, offering valuable experiences that shaped my career trajectory. Finally, landing a rewarding job as an account manager with Alcon was a realization of professional aspirations aligned with personal values. The role not only provided stability and growth opportunities but also resonated with my passion for eye care and helping others improve their quality of life. This resonated deeply with me because my career trajectory would have been vastly different if I hadn't prioritized getting my eyes checked for clear vision while playing as mentioned in my first book. Each of these milestones, occurring almost serendipitously within the same timeframe, wove together a narrative of personal and professional evolution. They were not just checkboxes ticked off but moments of profound significance, shaping my identity, purpose, and direction in life. This period stands as a testament to resilience, faith, and the power of perseverance amidst life's diverse challenges and opportunities.

Sharing these personal triumphs wasn't to boast but to illuminate that even in life's darkest moments, there's a potential for profound change and as you continue to read, you'll see why I took a moment to reflect on those moments. Our sauna encounter became a catalyst for mutual encouragement and empowerment that ended in prayer, proving that resilience and determination can pave paths to brighter futures, no matter how daunting the present may seem. Before we move too far ahead, let's rewind a bit to the prayer and delve into what unfolded after my initial retirement from football. It marked the culmination of a successful interim season with an emerging franchise called i9 Sports. The journey of revamping a youth sports program alongside family and friends was not without its share of joys and challenges.

Despite encountering occasional internal hiccups, our collective maturity prevailed as we set aside differences to prioritize the children's experiences, ensuring they had the best possible time. Our league encompassed a wide range of sports including soccer, tee-ball, basketball, cheerleading, and flag football, catering to children aged 3 to 14. Every weekend, we had the privilege of engaging with and serving over 200 enthusiastic kids across multiple venues. Despite the enormity of the task and the inevitable challenges, we were committed to showing up consistently and providing them with valuable tools that extended far beyond the immediate moment, shaping their lives for years to come. Our goal wasn't just to facilitate games and activities but to impart lasting lessons and skills that would stay with them throughout their lifetime, fostering growth, resilience, and a love for sports and teamwork. Through dedicated coaching, mentorship, and a nurturing environment, we aimed to instill qualities like discipline, teamwork, sportsmanship, and perseverance, equipping them not only for the games they played with us but also for the broader journey of life ahead. Seeing the positive impact on these young minds and witnessing their growth and development was not just rewarding but also a testament to the importance of investing in our youth and empowering them with tools they can carry into adulthood.

As we wrapped up the first season, packing up equipment and preparing to celebrate our achievements, a sudden twist emerged. My partner dropped the bombshell that she wouldn't be joining us for the celebration. Initially brushing it off as a jest, I urged her to stop teasing and join the festivities, unaware of the seriousness etched on her face. Her unexpected revelation—that she was embarking on a girl's trip with a few wives of my former teammates—left me stunned and bewildered. Questions swirled in my mind. Why reveal this plan on such a pivotal day? And why choose to depart precisely when our team was coming together to celebrate a milestone? These queries tugged at my heart as I navigated the complexities of this unforeseen turn of events.

Amidst this personal turmoil, my retirement from football emerged as a significant milestone. It signified not just the end of a chapter but also the beginning of introspection and reevaluation, prompting me to confront life's uncertainties with newfound resolve and clarity. Throughout my career journey, I encountered the delicate task of collaborating with family members, with whom harmony wasn't always immediate, contrasting with the relatively smoother dynamics of working alongside friends. One pivotal day, a comment from my partner struck a familiar chord, prompting me to seek clarification. Her words painted a picture of my perpetual absence—always on the go, leaving the family behind. I was immediately filled with agitation upon hearing the remark because it brought to mind the sacrifices I had personally made. Countless pivotal moments in my children's lives had been missed due to those sacrifices, and the remark felt ungrateful given the context. It's not just about being physically present; it's about the emotional toll and effort put into balancing work and family, a delicate dance many of us struggle with.

Sometimes, comments like that fail to appreciate the larger context of the sacrifices we make daily. Now that I was present, she expressed a need for a breather, rightfully so. While I understood her desire for space, I couldn't help but feel that comparing my work commitments to my familial presence was somewhat unfair. It highlighted the importance of effective communication in addressing such concerns. It's crucial to recognize the multifaceted nature of our responsibilities and find ways to balance them while ensuring that our loved ones feel valued and understood. This experience underscored the significance of open dialogue and mutual understanding in navigating complex situations like these. Our ensuing conversation brimmed with tension, casting a tense environment felt by those around us. As we continued, I urged everyone to carry on with plans as I resolved to address the matter privately later. Little did I realize the rapid unfolding of events; her departure, unknown to me until the last moment, left me questioning the spontaneity of a supposedly planned girl's trip.

As I made my way to join loved ones at the restaurant, the absence of my partner raised eyebrows and concern. Explaining the situation led to a collective surprise and immediate outreach to ensure her well-being. Amidst the camaraderie and shared meals, the absence lingered, prompting inquiries from our children during the ride back home. Navigating their concerns with care, I painted a reassuring picture of her temporary absence due to a work commitment, promising undivided attention to them in her absence. This unexpected turn of events marked a period of reflection and adaptation, underlining the complexities of balancing personal and professional spheres while nurturing familial bonds. We were all eagerly anticipating some much-needed quality time together, a rarity due to the demands of my bustling career, which took a toll on me mentally, emotionally, and physically. It was a chance to reconnect on a deeper level and create lasting memories that I had missed during my time away. As her trip commenced, I naturally wanted to ensure her safety and well-being, reaching out to no avail until she eventually messaged me back late that night, citing a dead phone battery but confirming her safe arrival. Despite her reassurances, an uneasy feeling lingered. The following day, my attempts at communication were met with silence, save for a brief message emphasizing her need for solitary writing time, devoid of distractions. Initially, from what was stated, I had assumed she was embarking on a fun getaway with friends, but her sudden shift towards solitude raised eyebrows even more.

Seeking reassurance and validity of her words, I decided to check with my former teammates about their wives' whereabouts, finding them all at home contrary to her claims. What began as a suspicion that this trip might not be genuine turned out to be true after I confirmed it with my friends. The realization hit me harder than I expected, and it stirred up a mix of emotions—disappointment, frustration, and a tinge of betrayal. It was a stark reminder that not everyone operates with honesty and integrity, and it made me reevaluate the trust I placed in certain relationships. This discrepancy raised concerns and triggered my mind to delve into the worst-case scenarios, grappling with intrusive thoughts about the possibility of infidelity. It was a distressing time as I wrestled with doubts and fears about the trustworthiness of the situation and the people involved. I had to navigate through these turbulent thoughts and emotions, trying to find clarity amidst the uncertainty. Despite my efforts to quiet such anxieties, a haunting dream or vision plagued my sleep that night, jolting me awake at 3:00 am, my heart racing and tears streaming down my face.

This turbulent episode marked a poignant intersection of doubt, worry, and a quest for truth, underscoring the fragile nature of trust and the unpredictable twists life can unveil even amidst seemingly ordinary circumstances. After retiring from football, I expected to return home and continue building on what I had started years ago. However, the current situation made me second-guess my decision to leave the game, especially since I knew I still had much more to offer. I found myself questioning whether I had made the right choice by retiring when I still had plenty of energy and talent to contribute.

To validate whether my unsettling experience was just a nightmare or reality, I turned to our family tracker app, hoping it was just my intrusive thoughts. What I discovered sent shockwaves through me as my eyebrows raised in suspense—multiple movements traced to different hotels, clubs, and bars. My attempt to reach her was met with more unanswered calls and texts, intensifying my restless night as intrusive thoughts flooded my mind. I said a prayer, seeking rest and asking for the strength to not bear the burden alone, as the weight of my thoughts was becoming too heavy to carry on my own. The following day brought no relief; calls and texts went unanswered, except for a fleeting moment of accidental connection where background noises hinted at festivities. This brief glimpse heightened my concerns, but clarity remained elusive until an unexpected message from a former colleague shed a little light on what was going on there. He casually mentioned crossing paths with her, painting a false picture of a museum visit—an unlikely scenario given her preferences. It became clear that a cover-up was in play. I've known this person for almost 20 years, and in all that time, I've never known her to show interest in visiting a museum. When I received that message, it immediately raised suspicions for me.

Despite feeling turmoil inside, I decided to exercise restraint and acknowledge the limits of control I had over her actions. It brought to mind something a coach often told us: "Control what you can, and don't worry about what you can't." Of course, putting that into practice proved to be much more challenging in this particular situation. Her return, marked by a palpable change in demeanor, spoke volumes. Coldness replaced warmth, and her words dripped with hostility, irritation, and avoidance. Attempts to address my concerns were met with dismissal and deflection, leaving me questioning my own perceptions amidst the growing rift. It was a bittersweet moment when the kids expressed joy at seeing her while I struggled with a mix of emotions. On one hand, their happiness brought a sense of relief and warmth, seeing them connecting with someone they cared about. However, beneath the surface lay a complex tangle of feelings. There was a growing sense of distance between us that seemed to widen with each passing interaction, and it weighed heavily on my mind. The internal struggle was palpable—a battle between the urge to step away from the situation, perhaps to protect myself emotionally, and the desire to stay, primarily for the sake of the kids. It was a delicate balance between personal needs and parental responsibilities, each pulling in opposite directions. As much as I wanted to maintain a unified front for the children's sake, the strain was undeniable. Navigating this emotional terrain required a tremendous amount of patience, self-reflection, and understanding. I had to constantly remind myself of the bigger picture, prioritizing the well-being and stability of our family unit. It was a journey of introspection, evaluating what truly mattered and finding ways to bridge the emotional gaps without compromising my own well-being.

A timely church sermon on infidelity and reconciliation about a week later felt like a divine intervention, nudging me towards an impending truth. As the testimonial unfolded, tears cascaded down my cheeks, a premonition of impending revelations. The air thickened with unspoken truths, setting the stage for an emotional storm brewing beneath, hinting at painful confrontations and uncharted territories of healing and forgiveness. It's amazing how certain sermons can resonate deeply within us, touching the hearts of many individuals simultaneously. In this instance, there was a sermon that seemed tailor-made for my situation, speaking directly to my inner struggles and offering a glimmer of hope. The message felt like a lifeline, something to cling to amidst the stormy seas of doubt and uncertainty.

However, as much as I wanted to embody the strength and conviction preached in those words, the reality of my personal situation loomed large. The sermon spoke of faith, resilience, and unwavering trust in divine providence. Yet, the very essence of those teachings felt challenged by the doubts and suspicions swirling in my mind during her absence. It's a unique kind of inner conflict—one where the ideals we hold dear clash with the harshness of reality. Believing in something wholeheartedly is one thing but living it out in the face of doubts and uncertainties is an entirely different challenge. I grappled with the discrepancy between what I aspired to be and the doubts that threatened to undermine that vision. At times, it felt like a test of faith in more ways than one. Could I uphold the principles I deeply believed in, even when faced with doubts and unsettling thoughts? The sermon's impact lingered, urging me to find strength and conviction, yet the practical application of those teachings seemed daunting in the face of personal turmoil.

This inner struggle highlighted the complexities of navigating faith and personal challenges, reminding me that belief isn't always a smooth, linear journey. It requires grappling with doubts, facing uncertainties head-on, and finding a way to reconcile our beliefs with the harsh realities of life. When we settled into the car after church, I broached the topic of the sermon and the testimonial we'd just heard. Her response was brief, a simple acknowledgment that it was just "good". As we sat in that charged silence, grappling with unspoken tensions, I wrestled with the weight of the impending conversation. Despite my initial reluctance, the emotional turmoil inside me demanded a voice. The air felt thick with unspoken truths as I prepared to drive away. Before I could start the car and put it in drive, she halted me with a confession. The atmosphere was heavy with unspoken emotions, and my struggle was evident, etched on my face.

Since her return, our home had become a landscape of unspoken tensions. Sleeping in separate rooms and strained interactions marked our days, hinting at an underlying rupture I feared confronting. The revelation she shared about the vivid dream I had experienced left me speechless, similarly to the shock of a sudden NFL team cut. As I grappled with the magnitude of the situation, a torrent of questions flooded my mind, each more agonizing than the last. Doubts about my worth, my abilities as a person, the stability of our family, and the future of our home loomed large, a cascade of uncertainty and pain like an "unnecessary roughness" penalty, where I felt blindsided and defenseless. Unlike the structured support system of my professional career, this personal crisis left me adrift, devoid of guidance or solace. Reflecting on the past often has a way of bringing forth emotions and memories we thought were long buried. It's like revisiting a familiar place only to find that the shadows of past experiences still linger, coloring our present perceptions.

The memory of being cut from a team, despite giving it your all and believing you were doing everything right, is undoubtedly a profound one. It's a moment that shakes the foundations of one's confidence and leaves you questioning not just your abilities but also the fairness of the situation. Those emotions and thoughts rushed back to the surface, echoing the frustrations and confusion of that time. I scrutinized every action, every practice session, and every game in search of answers. How could it be that despite my dedication and hard work, things didn't turn out as expected? It's a disorienting experience, especially when I was called in the office and was blindsided by an outcome that seem unjust or unexplained.

The struggle to process those emotions is a common thread among many who face similar situations. It's a mix of disbelief, disappointment, and perhaps even anger. I questioned my own perceptions, wondering if there was something I missed or if there were factors beyond my control at play. It's also a moment of introspection, where I got to evaluate not just the external circumstances but also my internal responses. Let me ask you this: How did you cope with that disappointment? Did it fuel a sense of determination to prove yourself elsewhere, or did it leave lingering doubts and insecurities?

Navigating through such experiences is as much about emotional resilience as it is about skill and talent. It's about finding ways to process and learn from setbacks, even when they seem unjust or bewildering. While the emotions may still linger, they also offer valuable insights into your growth journey— highlighting areas of strength, resilience, and perhaps areas that need further nurturing and development. The absence of a mentor figure or paternal advice compounded my feelings of failure and pushed me toward isolation. My attempts to find clarity through self-reflection and relentless self-improvement routines felt futile in the face of this emotional storm. Navigating this tumultuous chapter in my life was new as I was beginning to walk into uncharted territory. The fear of judgment, coupled with a lack of trust in confidants, left me feeling stranded in a sea of turmoil. My purpose, once driven by a desire to provide for my family, now seemed hollow against the backdrop of this unforeseen rupture.

As I grappled with conflicting emotions and sought solace in self-reflection, I clung to the belief that unity and resilience would prevail, even in the middle of chaos threatening to tear my world apart. Many nights found me in my closet, tears mingling with questions directed at God, seeking understanding amidst the turmoil. It was during these moments of despair that a gentle reminder of my prayers and divine presence brought comfort, soothing the anguish within. Self-blame crept in as I witnessed the unfolding of events I had fervently prayed against. The fear of becoming another statistic haunted me—I refused to succumb to divorce or resignation. Determined to salvage our marriage, I initiated discussions about counseling, recognizing the need for professional guidance in navigating our challenges, especially since we had never undergone premarital or any other form of counseling together.

Her initial reluctance and pessimism stung, but I clung to optimism, highlighting stories of resilience and renewal in other couples. Our conversations revolved around the sermon's message of hope and the transformative power of commitment to the healing process. Despite initial resistance, we tentatively agreed to counseling, hoping to mend what seemed irreparable. The counseling sessions, however, were marred by her silence and detachment, casting a pall of disillusionment over our efforts. Witnessing her disengagement, I felt my own resolve wane, the distance between us widening with each session. The grieving process unfolded predictably—from denial and anger to bargaining and depression—as I grappled with the reality of our situation. Ultimately, acceptance emerged from the depths of my heartache, paving the way for a painful yet necessary decision. The journey from hope to resignation was a tumultuous one, marked by a profound realization of personal limits and the inevitability of letting go in the face of insurmountable obstacles as I finally accepted it. Deciding to walk away from a situation, especially one I've invested significant time and effort into, was not easy. It spoke volumes about my strength and self-awareness to recognize when a situation was no longer serving my well-being.

The realization that staying in that environment wasn't conducive to a healthy home life weighed heavily on my heart. When my emotional and mental health were compromised, it was a clear sign that something needed to change. It took courage to acknowledge these truths, especially when I prided myself on perseverance and dedication.

I've never been one to quit easily, which reflects a commendable trait of resilience and commitment. However, there came a point when holding on became detrimental rather than beneficial. It was like realizing that continuing down a certain path only led to further exhaustion and emotional strain, despite my best efforts to weather the storm. The decision to let go and embark on a new journey signified a willingness to prioritize my well-being and emotional health. It was a pivot towards self-care and self-respect, acknowledging that my happiness and peace of mind mattered profoundly.

While endings can be challenging and bittersweet, they also pave the way for new beginnings and fresh opportunities. It's an acknowledgment that growth often requires us to step out of our comfort zones and embrace change, even when it comes with uncertainty.

Beginning anew carries a sense of hope and anticipation. It's a chance to create a healthier environment, nurture my emotional well-being, and validate my own feelings and experiences. It's about moving forward with lessons learned, resilience gained, and a renewed sense of purpose and direction. My willingness to make this choice speaks volumes about my courage and determination to prioritize what truly matters in life. It's a reminder that sometimes the bravest thing we can do is to let go of what no longer serves us and embrace the possibilities of a brighter tomorrow.

CHAPTER 2: FALSE START

It is a false start if there is any quick abrupt movement by a single offensive player, or by several offensive players in unison, which simulates the start of the snap, is a false start.

Navigating turbulent waters, I found myself grappling with an unexpected storm that tested the very foundation of my marriage and financial stability. The tempest began innocuously enough—a decision born from goodwill and a desire to support a friend embarking on his accounting career journey. Entrusting him with my tax filings seemed like a mutually beneficial arrangement, fostering his growth while ensuring my obligations were met. However, what ensued was a saga of challenges that pushed me to my limits and reshaped my perspective on trust and resilience. For two years, my friend diligently handled my taxes, weaving through complex financial regulations with what I believed was careful attention. It was during the second year that cracks began to surface, revealing errors that would have profound consequences. Letters from the IRS arrived ominously, bearing news of substantial debts that threatened to unravel years of financial prudence.

FALSE START

The subsequent meetings with IRS auditors felt like traversing a complex legal maze, where every question delved into intricate financial details with relentless precision. Frantically, I scoured my home, rifling through drawers for receipts, meticulously sifting through emails, and carefully examining every bank statement, all in an attempt to reconcile the numbers on the return with what had been filed. The weight of owing significant sums weighed heavily on my shoulders, challenging my belief in fiscal responsibility. Amidst the financial turmoil, emotions ran high, and blame became a tempting refuge for frayed nerves. Realizing my part in the situation, I reflected on how I had neglected my responsibility to thoroughly review what was filed. I had blindly placed my trust and electronically signed, acting with immaturity and without due diligence. Resentment simmered towards my friend whose inadvertent errors had triggered a domino effect of financial and emotional repercussions.

The impact extended beyond monetary liabilities, seeping into personal relationships like a noxious gas. Trust, once unwavering, fractured under the weight of financial missteps. It was a crucible that tested bonds, revealing strengths and vulnerabilities alike. Certain relationships endured the tempest, strengthened by shared empathy and deep understanding. However, for others, the stormy weather revealed hidden fault lines that had remained concealed for far too long. These fault lines, once exposed, led to fractures and ruptures, ultimately undermining the foundations of those relationships. This blindsided me and delivered a blow I didn't need amidst the storm I was already weathering. This was a person in need of a place to stay, and in an attempt to be godly and compassionate, I opened my home to him. He was finishing school, and I supported his business endeavors, even bringing others into the fold. I felt a deep sense of responsibility for everything that ensued, believing my decisions had repercussions for everyone involved.

However, his lack of consideration soon placed me in a difficult bind. I had taken a chance on him with being an assumed trust person, hoping to provide a stable environment and help him succeed. Instead, he took advantage of my kindness, causing unforeseen complications that added to my existing burdens. The situation quickly spiraled out of control, and I found myself grappling with the consequences of my well-intentioned actions. My intent was to embody the principles of generosity and support, to act in a way that aligned with my faith and values. But instead of gratitude and mutual respect, I was met with disregard and irresponsibility. The strain of managing this situation, on top of my already overwhelming challenges, was nearly too much to bear. It felt like a betrayal. I had extended my hand in friendship and support, only to have it slapped away by someone I trusted. This lack of consideration for my circumstances and the added pressure it brought into my life were disheartening. I had hoped to create a positive and supportive environment, but instead, I found myself entangled in a web of complications that tested my patience and resilience.

FALSE START

Reflecting on this, I realized the importance of setting boundaries and being discerning about who I allow into my personal space. While my intentions were noble, I learned that not everyone appreciates or respects such gestures. This experience taught me a hard lesson about the balance between helping others and protecting my own well-being. It was a harsh reminder that even in acts of kindness, one must be vigilant and mindful of the potential consequences. In hindsight, it was a reminder of the importance of resilience and effective communication in navigating turbulent times. Yet, amidst adversity, seeds of resilience and growth were sown. I found myself reassessing priorities, strengthening financial literacy, and rebuilding trust on firmer ground. The experience, though arduous, became a catalyst for personal and relational growth. It highlighted the importance of due diligence, open communication, and seeking professional expertise where necessary. As I reflect on those challenging times, I am reminded of the silver linings that emerged from the dark clouds of uncertainty. While the scars remain, they serve as reminders of lessons learned and paths forged anew.

Adversity, though daunting, can be a crucible for transformation and growth, shaping character and fortitude in unexpected ways. Drawing a parallel to sports, where an ill-timed move incurs penalties, I reflected on my situation as a 'false start'—acting prematurely despite knowing the play, leading to dire consequences. A false start by an offensive player is one of the most avoidable mistakes in football because it directly involves mental focus and discipline. As a player, you know the snap count intimately. You've practiced it relentlessly, day in and day out, and it's drilled into you during every huddle before the play. If the pressure feels overwhelming or you find yourself distracted, the simplest advice is to watch the ball and not move until you see it snapped.

In my situation, however, focus was elusive. This season of my life was a blur, clouded by the weight of legal troubles with the IRS. Despite my best efforts to comply with tax regulations, I discovered that I had inadvertently broken the law, facing the harrowing possibility of jail time. The stakes were high, and the stress was palpable. This period felt like one prolonged false start. Every attempt to move forward was marred by missteps and setbacks. Just as in football, where a false start can derail an entire play, my lack of focus and the ensuing legal complications threatened to unravel everything I had worked for. Navigating through the maze of IRS regulations and legal requirements was daunting. The fear of incarceration loomed large, a constant reminder of the precariousness of my situation. It was a time of intense pressure, akin to the moments before the snap in a critical game, but infinitely more consequential. The stakes weren't just the outcome of a game; they were my freedom, my future, and the stability of my family.

Looking back, the lessons from the football field seemed almost prophetic. The importance of focus, discipline, and staying grounded under pressure were not just athletic virtues

FALSE START

but life-saving skills. Just as a false start in a game teaches you the importance of mental preparation and resilience, my legal ordeal underscored the need for meticulous attention to detail and unwavering determination. In the end, this tumultuous period reinforced the value of vigilance and the dire consequences of losing focus, whether on the field or in life. It was a harsh but necessary lesson, one that has left an indelible mark on my approach to both personal and professional challenges. The financial strain cascaded into a series of losses, facing the dissolution of my marriage, the looming possibility of not having full-time custody of my kids, the potential loss of the youth league that had brought me so much joy, the foreclosure of my home, and the rapid depletion of my finances left me in an incredibly dire and vulnerable situation. It felt like the pillars of my life were crumbling around me, and I struggled to find solid ground amidst the chaos. Each of these challenges weighed heavily on my mind and heart, amplifying my sense of despair and uncertainty about the future.

The ensuing chaos propelled me into survival mode, grappling with the erosion of my credit score, imminent financial ruin, and the emotional toll of shattered dreams and strained relationships. The weight of embarrassment and a perceived loss of identity as a pillar of strength compounded my challenges, leaving me adrift without a lifeline. Amid this turmoil, a glimmer of hope emerged through an unexpected opportunity—the NFL's business symposium in Arizona tailored for former players transitioning post-football. This comprehensive program offered vital resources, mentorship, and potential job prospects, rekindling a spark of optimism through the darkest chapter of my life. Navigating adversity, I learned resilience, humility, and the importance of seeking support during life's toughest trials. The symposium marked a pivotal turning point, reigniting hope and paving a path toward rebuilding despite the ruins of financial and personal devastation. I saw the NFL symposium as a potential lifeline to halt my financial decline, so I promptly booked a flight in hopes of securing a job or at least gaining clarity on my next steps. The experience surpassed my expectations; reconnecting with former teammates who were also in dire straits reminded me that my struggles weren't isolated.

As former players took the stage, sharing candid accounts of their struggles and the invaluable support they received from the NFL, a sense of camaraderie permeated the room. It was a poignant reminder of the brotherhood forged on the field, a bond that transcended the game itself. Yet, as life outside the confines of the locker room unfolded, the dynamics shifted. The unity and solidarity that once defined our collective experience gave way to a blunt reality: the harsh individualism of the outside world. It felt as though we were thrust back into the wilderness of competition, where survival depended solely on one's own prowess. The relationships that had once anchored us during our playing days began to fade, their once-strong foundations crumbling beneath the weight of distance and diverging paths. What remained was a facade of familiarity, devoid of the deep-rooted connections that once bound us together. In the absence of genuine companionship, I found myself adrift in a sea of solitude. The camaraderie that had sustained us through the rigors of professional sports was now a distant memory, replaced by an unsettling sense of isolation.

It was a sobering realization, one that underscored the transient nature of human connections and the fleeting nature of fame. As I navigated this newfound sense of aloneness, I couldn't help but yearn for the camaraderie of the locker room, where bonds were forged in the crucible of competition and adversity. On the pivotal day of interviews, I made a promising connection with Riddell, a company in search of an immediate sales rep. Their offer included a relocation package, signifying a fresh start but also signaling potential upheaval for my family and home in Texas. Despite the uncertainties, their interest in me and my urgent need for income compelled me to consider the offer seriously. Though initially hesitant, I requested a day to weigh the pros and cons. Realizing the gravity of my situation, I understood that there was no feasible way for me to sustain the life I had been building. The burden of the mortgage payments weighed heavily on my finances, pushing them beyond their limits. At the same time, I grappled with the pressing need to provide adequately for my children, which seemed increasingly unattainable given my financial constraints. Faced with these unbellished realities, the decision to let go of the home became a clear and pragmatic choice. It was a painful but necessary step to ensure that my children's needs could continue to be met, even if it meant relinquishing a place that held so many memories and aspirations.

After careful contemplation, I accepted Riddell's offer, a decision that meant uprooting from Texas to Detroit. Packing up and leaving was bittersweet; I confided in my cousin about the job opportunity without divulging the full extent of my circumstances. Leaving our home and navigating through life's uncertainties weighed heavily on me as a parent. The decisions I had to make felt like a constant battle between what was necessary for our survival and the emotional toll it took on my children. Each move brought with it waves of change, disrupting the stability they had grown accustomed to. It was heartbreaking to see them uprooted from familiar surroundings, separated from friends they had grown close to, and having to adjust to new schools repeatedly. Witnessing the impact on my children's lives was one of the most challenging aspects to bear. Their resilience was admirable, but it pained me to see them endure these transitions, knowing that they were missing out on the continuity and security every child deserves.

As a parent, it was a constant struggle between providing for their immediate needs and striving to create a sense of stability and normalcy amidst the upheaval. These experiences made me question my decisions and wonder if there could have been better alternatives. The guilt of putting them through such life changing events gnawed at me, and I often second-guessed whether I was making the right choices for their well-being.

FALSE START

Despite the difficulties, I tried my best to be a source of strength and reassurance for them, emphasizing the importance of resilience and adaptability in life's ever-changing journey. With my cousin's help, we embarked on the long journey to Detroit, where we temporarily settled with family while scouting for a more permanent residence.

Transitioning to Detroit brought with it a whirlwind of emotions, a symphony of anticipation and trepidation that played out in every decision I made. The job I secured at Riddell provided a much-needed anchor of stability in turbulent seas, offering financial respite while I navigated the stormy waters of life. However, beneath the surface of this newfound stability lay the submerged wreckage of painful memories and unresolved familial discord that haunted the cityscape of Detroit. Its streets echoed with echoes of past struggles, reminding me of battles fought and scars borne. Amidst this backdrop of inner turmoil and external stability, my days at Riddell unfolded in a tapestry of connections old and new. The work not only allowed me to hone my professional skills but also rekindled relationships with local schools, coaches, and long-lost friends. Each encounter brought a sense of familiarity in an otherwise alien environment, weaving a thread of continuity through the fabric of change. Yet, even as I settled into my role and routines, the nights in Detroit became moments of introspection and fervent prayers, seeking solace and divine guidance in the midst of uncertainties that loomed like shadows.

Foremost among these uncertainties were the nagging questions about the future — where would I live, how would I sustain myself, and what did this mean for my relationship with my children? The fear of the unknown cast a long shadow, its tendrils creeping into every corner of my thoughts. It was a time of soul-searching, a crucible where the desire for stability clashed with the allure of escape from the ghosts of the past that haunted me in Detroit. Amidst these contemplations, my first strategic move was to secure a place to call my own. The search for an apartment became not just a quest for shelter but a metaphorical journey towards self-reliance and renewal. Providence intervened unexpectedly, presenting an opportunity despite my financial red flags. Open and honest conversations with an apartment manager became pivotal in navigating the challenges I faced during that time. I found that sharing my struggles and being transparent about my circumstances not only helped me to express my concerns but also fostered a sense of understanding and empathy from the manager's side.

During these candid discussions, I detailed the financial hardships and uncertainties I was grappling with, highlighting the urgency and importance of securing a stable living situation for myself and my family. I explained the impact of recent life changes and how they had affected my ability to meet traditional housing criteria, such as credit scores or income thresholds. To my relief, the apartment manager showed a remarkable level of empathy and willingness to work with me. Instead of rigidly adhering to strict policies, they listened attentively,

FALSE START

acknowledged the challenges I faced, and offered assurances that they would do their best to assist in the approval process. This understanding approach not only eased my anxieties but also provided a glimmer of hope during an otherwise stressful period. Their assurances were not just verbal; they followed through by expediting necessary paperwork, offering flexible leasing options, and demonstrating a genuine desire to help me secure a stable living environment. This collaborative effort between myself and the apartment manager showed the power of empathy. Ultimately, this positive interaction with the apartment manager not only paved the way for approval but also instilled a sense of gratitude and appreciation for the human connection that transcended mere business transactions. It was a reminder that empathy and compassion can make a significant difference in people's lives, especially during challenging times.

However, with each step towards personal stability came the bittersweet task of communicating changes to my loved ones. Conversations with my children about moving out and establishing a new home carried the weight of their innocence amidst upheaval. Similarly, discussions with their mother about the irreconcilable nature of our differences marked the end of one chapter and the uncertain beginning of another. This transition was not just about changing addresses but about unearthing buried emotions and acknowledging the wounds that needed healing. It was a transformative period that demanded resilience and introspection, a journey towards understanding the depths of pain and the flickering hope of renewal that lay ahead on the horizon of life. Securing the apartment felt like a significant step toward reclaiming my independence and rebuilding my life. It was more than just finding a place to live; it was a tangible marker of progress toward self-sufficiency. For the first time in a long while, I felt a sense of forward momentum.

This victory provided a much-needed boost to my self-esteem, reminding me that I was capable of overcoming the obstacles that had been thrown my way. This achievement was particularly poignant given the emotional and physical distance from my children. Adjusting to a new norm without their constant presence was challenging, but securing a stable home was a crucial part of creating a foundation that would ultimately benefit them. Knowing that I had a safe and secure place to call my own gave me a renewed sense of purpose and direction.

This newfound stability allowed me to focus on other important areas of my life. With a roof over my head and a sense of security, I could channel my energy into my career, personal growth, and most importantly, maintaining strong connections with my children. The apartment symbolized a fresh start, an opportunity to build a life that I could be proud of and one that my children could look up to. The experience also taught me the value of perseverance and the importance of self-reliance. It reminded me that even in the face of adversity, it is possible to find a way forward. The path to self-sufficiency is often fraught with challenges, but each victory, no matter how small, is a step closer to the freedom and stability I sought. Ultimately, securing the apartment was not just a logistical victory; it was an emotional and psychological one as well. It marked the beginning of a new chapter in my life, one where I could build a solid foundation for my future and the future of my children. This milestone was a reminder that progress is possible, and that with determination and resilience, I could navigate the challenges ahead and create a better life for myself and my family.

CHAPTER 3: FIRST DOWN

A gain of ten or more yards by an offensive team entitles it to continued possession for a new series of downs.

Settling into my new apartment brought about a delicate balance of peace and unfamiliarity. While my role at Riddell was fulfilling and my job was progressing well, I often found myself contemplating the deeper meaning of my life's journey and how it intertwined with my current circumstances. I struggled with a profound sense of worthlessness, questioning how my life had spiraled to this point. Once a celebrated athlete, holding records at my high school, college, and even in the NFL and CFL, I now found myself living in a one-bedroom apartment, teetering on the edge of divorce, and facing severe financial troubles. My pride and ego were shattered, and the humiliation was almost unbearable.

Reflecting on this drastic fall from grace was a humbling experience. It was as if I had been riding a wave of success, only to be abruptly cast ashore by the harsh tides of reality. The accolades and achievements that once defined me seemed like distant echoes, overshadowed by the pressing challenges of my current situation. This period of adversity forced me to confront my vulnerabilities head-on. It was a severe reminder that no amount of past glory could shield me from the trials of the present. The isolation of my small apartment contrasted sharply with the bustling stadiums and adoring fans of my past. Each day was a struggle to reconcile my former identity with my current circumstances.

However, this humbling experience was necessary. It compelled me to slow down and reevaluate my priorities. The relentless pursuit of success had blinded me to the more profound aspects of life, and this setback provided a much-needed opportunity for introspection. It was a chance to redefine my sense of self-worth, no longer tethered to external accolades but rooted in a deeper understanding of resilience and personal growth. In the quiet moments of reflection, I began to see this chapter as a critical juncture in my journey. It was a time to rebuild, not just my financial stability, but also my sense of self. The struggles I faced became lessons in humility and perseverance. They taught me to value the intangible aspects of life—relationships, inner peace, and the strength to rise again.

Despite the positive momentum of securing a new job, a somewhat comfortable living space, and navigating parental responsibilities with my kids, there remained an inner longing for something more substantial. Although reconnecting with old friends and spending quality time with family provided temporary solace, a sense of emptiness persisted, casting shadows on my newfound stability. One seemingly ordinary day, as I scrolled through Instagram, a video featuring one of my former teammates caught my eye. He was thriving in Canada, setting records and basking in the glory of his accomplishments. The camaraderie, passion, and thrill evident in that video stirred a dormant desire within me—to return to the game I once loved. Witnessing him receive a game ball for breaking passing records ignited a fire in me, triggering vivid memories of my own days on the field. Despite initial doubts about revisiting my football career in Canada, a powerful dream that night seemed like a vision, urging me to explore this path once more.

Driven by newfound determination, I confided in a close friend about my dream and the resurfaced passion for football. Not only did my passion for the game resurface, but I realized that my identity was still deeply intertwined with it. Working a regular job felt foreign and unsettling. Beyond football, I felt adrift, uncertain of my true worth and value to others. From a young age, I had been celebrated as an athlete, and this abrupt transition, coupled with other painful changes, thrust me into an unfamiliar and uncomfortable position. Growing up, football was more than just a game—it was my identity, my refuge, and my pride. The field was where I found my sense of purpose and validation. Being an athlete defined my interactions, my relationships, and how I viewed myself. When the roar of the crowd faded, so did my sense of self. I was no longer the star player but just another person trying to find his way in a world that no longer revolved around my athletic prowess.

FIRST DOWN

The drastic change from being celebrated for my physical abilities to navigating the mundanity of a regular job was jarring. Each day at work felt like a reminder of what I had lost. I found myself yearning for the adrenaline, the camaraderie, and the sense of achievement that football provided. The daily grind lacked the passion and excitement that had fueled me for so long. It wasn't just a job—it felt like a diminishment of who I was. The other tumultuous changes in my life—my failing marriage, financial troubles, and the impending separation from my children—compounded my sense of disorientation. The stability I once took for granted crumbled, leaving me to confront questions I had never asked myself before. Who was I without football? What value did I bring to the table now that I was no longer in the spotlight? These were questions that haunted me, pushing me into a state of existential crisis.

This period of upheaval forced me to face a harsh reality. The accolades and achievements that once defined me were now memories. The transition was not just about finding a new career path; it was about rediscovering and redefining myself from the ground up. I had to learn to derive my sense of worth from within, independent of external validation and applause. It was a humbling experience that I wasn't ready for. It required me to strip away the layers of my former identity and build a new one based on values, relationships, and inner strength rather than accolades and public admiration. This journey of self-discovery was fraught with pain, confusion, and doubt, but it was also a necessary process. It was about finding balance, embracing change, and recognizing that my worth was not solely tied to my athletic achievements.

In retrospect, this period of turmoil was a crucial chapter in my life. It was about slowing down, reassessing my priorities, and putting things into perspective. It was about learning to value myself beyond my physical abilities and recognizing that my contributions and worth extended far beyond the football field. This painful transition was a steppingstone toward a more grounded, self-aware version of myself. I reached out to my former teammate from the video, expressing my interest in returning to the game and inquiring about a tryout opportunity. His surprised yet encouraging response mirrored my own determination, setting the wheels in motion for a potentially life-altering journey. The subsequent conversations with team management were filled with excitement and optimism, culminating in a swift contract offer and flight arrangements within a span of hours. My decision to keep this transformational chapter under wraps, known only to a trusted few, allowed me to focus wholeheartedly on this new adventure. As I embarked on the flight to Canada, leaving behind my apartment responsibilities temporarily under my cousin's watchful eye, a wave of anticipation and nostalgia washed over me. Arriving in Canada felt like a homecoming of sorts. The warm reception from coaches, teammates, and the passionate fan base enveloped me in a sense of belonging and purpose. The initial weeks were dedicated to rigorous training sessions and playbook studies, ensuring I was physically and mentally prepared for my imminent return to the field. Along with the whirlwind of excitement and personal fulfillment, a realization dawned on me about the unaddressed emotional trauma lingering from past experiences—an aspect of my life I had unwittingly neglected.

I didn't take the time to pause and process my feelings or emotions. Like I was taught in football and ingrained in me since boyhood, I simply brushed off the pain, metaphorically putting dirt on the wound, and kept moving forward. I adopted a mentality of relentless perseverance, never stopping to acknowledge the emotional toll of my experiences. It wasn't until I returned to Canada that the weight of my unprocessed emotions became undeniable. The familiar surroundings brought back a flood of memories, and I realized I couldn't continue to ignore the turmoil within. The facade of strength I had maintained began to crack, revealing the vulnerabilities I had long suppressed. In Canada, away from the constant demands and distractions, I had a moment of clarity. The memories of past victories and defeats, both on and off the field, resurfaced, and I found myself confronting feelings I had buried for years. The isolation provided a bleak contrast to the bustling life I was accustomed to, forcing me to face the emotional residue of my past.

It became clear that I needed to talk to someone about the things I had experienced and figure out where to place them. The accumulation of unresolved issues—from the pressures of being an athlete to the personal challenges I faced—had reached a tipping point. I recognized that seeking professional help was not a sign of weakness but a necessary step towards healing. Engaging with a therapist allowed me to unpack the emotional baggage I had been carrying. Through these conversations, I began to understand the importance of processing my feelings rather than just pushing through them. It was a journey of self-discovery, where I learned to acknowledge and validate my emotions instead of dismissing them. This process was transformative. I realized that true strength lay not in ignoring pain but in confronting it head-on. I learned to navigate my emotions, to understand their origins, and to find healthy ways to express and manage them. This period of introspection and therapy was crucial in helping me rebuild my mental and emotional resilience.

Returning to Canada and seeking help marked a turning point in my life. It taught me the value of emotional honesty and the importance of mental health. No longer did I feel the need to mask my struggles with a veneer of toughness. Instead, I embraced a more holistic approach to well-being, understanding that mental and emotional health were as vital as physical strength. This journey not only helped me heal but also was preparing me to face future challenges with a more balanced and healthier mindset. As my journey in Canada progressed positively, with genuine care and support surrounding me, an unforeseen complication arose back in the States. Riddell, understandably protective of their professional commitments, initiated a conversation about my dual roles. Acknowledging the conflict of interest, we amicably parted ways, allowing me to fully immerse myself in this newfound football journey.

Reflecting on this transformative phase, I recognize the profound impact of embracing passions and navigating unexpected opportunities. This chapter in my life not only rekindled my love for football but also facilitated personal healing and growth. It serves as a testament to resilience, adaptability, and the unyielding pursuit of purpose, even when paths diverge unexpectedly. I found it rather ironic how my signing with the Saskatchewan Roughriders marked a full-circle moment in my Canadian football journey. Back in 2009, this was the first team I tried out for during my initial stint in Canada. However, I didn't make the cut back then. This time around, things felt different—I felt wanted, and I came with more valuable playing experience under my belt.

The announcement of my signing with the Saskatchewan Roughriders as a kick returner on September 12, 2017, brought a renewed sense of purpose. Despite only playing a few regular-season games, I made impactful contributions, showcasing my skills during crucial plays. For instance, during the 2017 Eastern Semi-final game in Ottawa, I delivered a stellar performance as a running back, earning significant rushing yards and even securing a memorable touchdown, among other notable plays that helped secure a victory for the team. Here's a clipping of an article for reference: *On September 12, 2017, the Saskatchewan Roughriders announced that they had signed Thigpen to their practice roster as a kick returner. Thigpen played in only two regular-season games for the Riders in 2017, carrying the ball seven times for 32 yards and catching two passes for 31 yards. He also returned two punts and one kick return. Playing mainly as a running back in the 2017 Eastern Semi-final game in Ottawa, he amassed 169 rushing yards, including a 75-yard touchdown, placing him third all-time for a Saskatchewan player in a playoff game. He also had 38 yards on two kickoff returns to help defeat the Ottawa Redblacks 31–20.*

Leaving my role at Riddell to pursue my football aspirations felt like the right move, especially after receiving recognition and positive feedback following the season. However, this decision also came with financial repercussions. Transitioning to a lower-paying job in football meant a significant pay cut. Adding to this challenge was the difference in currency values between the Canadian and American dollars, alongside associated fees for currency exchange and taxation. Despite returning home with a near-empty bank account, I remained optimistic about securing a contract for the next season. Navigating the financial uncertainties post-season led me to explore various job opportunities back home in Detroit. However, the search yielded limited results, prompting me to seek assistance from programs designed to support former NFL players facing hardships. The irony of finding myself in need despite being familiar with such financial aid programs wasn't lost on me. It served as a humbling reminder of the unpredictability of life after professional sports. I immediately thought of a valuable resource I had learned about during the event. I knew that the brief respite away in

Saskatchewan hadn't provided the financial stability I needed to sustain myself and manage my priorities until the next season.

This assistance would be crucial, offering a vital lifeline while I once again navigated the job market. The symposium had highlighted various support programs available to former athletes, and I wasted no time in applying for them. The knowledge I gained there proved to be indispensable, as it connected me with the financial aid necessary to keep afloat during this challenging period. Securing this assistance was a significant relief. It helped cover essential expenses, alleviating some of the financial pressure that had been mounting. With these funds, I could dedicate myself more fully to the task of securing stable employment, free from the immediate concern of how I would manage to maintain rent payments and essential utilities like electricity and running water in my apartment. The support provided a buffer, allowing me to regroup and plan my next steps more strategically. It was not just a financial boost but also an emotional one, giving me the confidence to persist in my job search and maintain hope for the future. This aid underscored the importance of utilizing available resources and highlighted the power of the network I had built through my connections at the symposium. This season of my life mirrored the earlier days when I juggled football alongside supplemental work, reminiscent of my time playing in Canada during my initial stint. The cyclical nature of this phase in my life was both unexpected and humbling. As I scoured for employment opportunities, finding myself falling short, I made the decision to turn to Lyft for a source of income. Its straightforward hiring process allowed me to start earning almost immediately. Driving became my daily grind, a means to pay the bills and provide extra support for my children. It was a harsh transition from my days as a professional football player to being alone behind the wheel, navigating the streets as a Lyft driver.

The experience was a blend of excitement and apprehension. Driving in Detroit, known for its safety concerns, compelled me to take precautions. I carried a firearm for protection, avoided late-night shifts, and sometimes had my cousin accompany me, even though it was technically against the rules. Despite the risks, driving for Lyft became my ministry on wheels, opening doors to profound conversations that touched my heart. One encounter that stands out vividly is when I picked up a young woman heading to a hair salon. As we drove, she opened up about her battle with a rare form of cancer. Learning that she was only 19 years old and had just six months to live struck a chord with me. Despite her grim prognosis, she faced her situation with remarkable courage and acceptance. Her strength and unwavering faith left a lasting impact on me, reminding me of the resilience of the human spirit. I offered to pray for her and stayed in touch, even keeping my word to bring her my first published book when I finished writing it. I stayed in touch and witnessing her miraculous recovery was a testament to the power of faith and perseverance. Her victory over cancer serves as a beacon of hope, a reminder that even in our darkest moments, there is always a glimmer of light. Through her story,

I learned the importance of holding onto hope and trusting the journey, no matter how challenging it may seem. It's a testament to the resilience of the human spirit and the transformative power of faith. As I share her story, I hope to inspire others to believe in the possibility of miracles and to never lose hope, no matter how dire the circumstances may appear.

Driving for Lyft was consuming too much of my time and wasn't yielding the financial stability I required, although it did provide some assistance. What made matters worse during my financial challenges, I found myself making regrettable personal decisions, particularly in relationships. Ignoring moral convictions in pursuit of temporary satisfaction led to unintended consequences, including strained relationships and unexpected fatherhood. These personal struggles compounded the financial pressures, highlighting a critical period of self-reflection and growth. As I grappled with financial and relational turmoil, I acknowledged the need for introspection and change. Confronting past mistakes and the repercussions of impulsive decisions, I embarked on a journey of personal growth and accountability. This period marked a transformative chapter defined by resilience, humility, and the pursuit of a more balanced and purposeful life both on and off the field. In hindsight, I must admit I didn't handle things as courageously or responsibly as I should have. Instead of facing my problems head-on, like a man of faith should, I chose the path of avoidance and escapism. It's a painful chapter in my life, one that I'm still learning from every day. I met these two different women a year apart and my unhealed trauma and unresolved issues led me to handle these relationships in terrible ways. I failed to meet my responsibilities as a man and a father. As I look back, I'm haunted by the memory of my departure, realizing I wasn't there to share in the journey of pregnancy and childbirth with them. I failed to offer the support they rightfully deserved, and the weight of that realization fills me with profound regret and sorrow. I'm not seeking pity or absolution for my shortcomings; rather, I'm choosing to open up and be vulnerable about this aspect of my journey. It's important for me to acknowledge and reflect on how poorly I handled myself and others during this challenging season of my life.

Looking back, I see how my own wounds and insecurities clouded my judgment and hindered my ability to be there for them in the way they needed. Instead of facing my demons head-on and seeking healing, I allowed them to dictate my actions, causing irreparable harm to them and the residual effects that still linger today. It's a crucial reminder of the importance of addressing our past traumas and seeking help when needed. I've come to understand that running away from our problems only amplifies them, affecting not only ourselves but also those around us. My journey has taught me the value of accountability and the necessity of confronting our inner demons to prevent history from repeating itself. While I can't change the past, I'm committed to making amends and being a better partner and father moving forward. It's a journey of self-discovery and growth, one that I'm navigating with humility and a newfound determination to break the cycle of pain and dysfunction. This led me back to Canada, where I attempted to erase the life I built, fueled in part by troubling rumors about paternity (which was the easy way out) and other personal matters that haunted my thoughts daily. I carried these burdens onto the football field, where each game and practice felt like a gamble with fate due to my own internal conflicts, despite my desire to live a righteous life.

As a Christian, I grappled with feelings of spiritual lukewarmness, a state I considered among the worst in my journey with faith. I knew I wasn't setting the best example back home; I was acutely aware of the responsibilities I abandoned, yet I attempted to bury them deep within, hoping they would fade away. The burden of guilt and shame weighed heavily on me, often leaving me feeling undeserving of God's protection. Yet, in my failings and disobedience, I found solace in God's grace, realizing that despite my shortcomings, He remained faithful. The football season brought success on the field, yet off-field uncertainties loomed large. During this season, I experienced a remarkable peak in my career, defying the constraints of age and tirelessly striving to outpace Father Time. Despite the inevitable march of years, I remained steadfast in my dedication to the game, pouring every ounce of effort into maintaining peak performance. The accolades I garnered as the top kick returner were not merely a stroke of luck but a testament to the countless hours of hard work and determination I invested. On the field, I was surging forward, gaining ground with every yard towards that elusive first down marker. Each play felt like a step closer to victory. But off the field, it was a different story entirely. Despite my efforts on the gridiron, I couldn't shake the feeling that I was losing ground elsewhere. It was as if for every yard gained on the field, I was losing ground in my personal life.

Off the field, my commitment to excellence manifested in rigorous training sessions that extended beyond scheduled practices. On off days, I could often be found in the weight room, pushing myself to the limits to build strength and endurance. Even after grueling practice sessions, I dedicated extra time to studying film, analyzing opponents' strategies, and refining my techniques. It was this relentless pursuit of improvement, coupled with an unwavering work ethic, that allowed me to achieve some of the longest breakaway runs of the season. Each stride down the field was not just a display of physical prowess but a culmination of meticulous preparation and unwavering focus. This season of my life served as a testament to the power of dedication and perseverance, proving that with determination, age is no barrier to greatness.

Despite the chaos, I clung to remnants of spiritual discipline, seeking solace in daily sermons and Bible readings. These moments offered a lifeline amid personal struggles and lapses in judgment. I knew deep down that there was more to life than mere survival; there was a call to meaningful change and growth that I couldn't ignore. Returning to Canada for another

FIRST DOWN

football season brought a mix of familiarity and relief. The community's warmth and passion for the team provided a comforting backdrop aside from life's uncertainties. However, even with the support, personal challenges continued to tug at my resolve, reminding me of the work still needed within myself. The seasonal rhythm of football brought brief respites, like our bye-week, offering time for physical and mental recuperation. Yet, even in these moments, the underlying struggles persisted, reminding me that true transformation required more than temporary breaks or escapes. As I navigated these complexities, the need for substantial changes in my life grew clearer. The familiar cycle of disappointment and unmet potential underscored the urgency of addressing internal and external challenges.

Each day became not just about surviving but actively seeking growth and redemption in every aspect of life. Experiencing a sudden turn of events during what was supposed to be a routine trip back to Detroit was unnerving, to say the least. The decision to visit family during our bye-week seemed like a well-deserved break to recharge before the upcoming demanding stretch of games. As I was flying back home, I was stopped, little did I know, that brief detour through Minnesota would lead to a distressing encounter at the airport. Being stopped by customs in Minnesota was unexpected and unsettling, especially since my documents were all in order. The lack of explanation from the officials added to the confusion. Returning home temporarily rejuvenated my spirits, but the determination to be fully prepared for the next series of games motivated me to return a few days earlier. However, what awaited me at the airport was far from any athletic preparation.

As I navigated through the airport, mundane tasks like boarding my flight turned into surreal encounters. A chance encounter with my coach headed back the same day on the same flight, conversation with my cousin over Air Pods, and the usual boarding process quickly spiraled into an unexpected confrontation with law enforcement. Approaching my gate for boarding, I exchanged pleasantries with the ticket agent, unaware of the impending disruption. Moments later, encountering law enforcement officers at the end of the jet bridge was a jarring reality check. Their abrupt request to confirm my identity and subsequent revelation about an outstanding warrant for unpaid child support caught me off guard, to say the least. The mix of emotions that surged through me – from shock to anxiety – was palpable. My mind raced with questions and concerns about the situation unfolding before me. Trying to convey the situation to my cousin over the phone while complying with the officers' instructions added to the tense atmosphere.

The surreal nature of being detained right before boarding a flight added an additional layer of disbelief. The sequence of events – from routine travel to an unexpected arrest – underscored the complexities of managing personal and professional responsibilities. It was a important reminder of the need for meticulous attention to legal matters and financial obligations, even amid demanding athletic careers. Although the circumstances were deeply troubling, having my cousin witness the encounter remotely provided a crucial lifeline. It highlighted the importance of having support systems in place during unforeseen crises. As unsettling as the experience was, it also served as a wake-up call. I've always been hesitant to embrace the concept of karma, but reflecting on my journey, I couldn't help but acknowledge the weight of my actions and their repercussions. The choices I made, the paths I walked, they all converged to bring me to this moment. There's a sense of inevitability in it, a feeling that I'm reaping what I've sown.

I've come to realize that the way I've conducted myself in the world has had profound implications on my circumstances. It's not just chance or happenstance that has led me here; rather, it's the culmination of my deeds, both good and bad. In many ways, I feel as though I deserve this. Not in a punitive sense, but rather as a natural consequence of my actions. I've had to confront the ways in which I've fallen short, the ways in which I've failed to live up to my own ideals. It's a sobering realization, but also a necessary one if I'm to move forward with integrity and purpose.

CHAPTER 4: UNSPORTSMANLIKE CONDUCT

Using abusive, threatening, or insulting language or gestures to opponents, teammates, officials, or representatives of the League. Using baiting or taunting acts or words that may engender ill will between teams.

I've had my fair share of moments where frustration got the better of me, especially in interactions with officials and coaches. I've voiced concerns over missed calls, only to realize later that my reactions weren't in line with who I am. These instances serve as reminders of how emotions can lead us astray. However, none of those experiences could have prepared me for the overwhelming embarrassment of being arrested on a public jet bridge. The scene of being handcuffed wasn't a simple hands-behind-the-back scenario; it was a deliberate process, chaining my hands in front of me and connecting them to shackles around my ankles. It felt like a deliberate attempt to showcase my predicament to everyone around. Walking back up the jet bridge with officers by my side, the stares of passengers and airport staff alike were suffocating. The unkempt state of my facial hair only added to the spectacle, compounding my sense of mortification. The ticket agent's shocked expression mirrored the collective astonishment of those witnessing the scene unfold. As I walked past, heads turned, conversations paused, and I felt the weight of judgment, gazes, and curiosity bear down on me. It was a humbling experience, one that forced me to confront my own actions and the consequences they carried.

Once inside the van, the absence of windows heightened my apprehension. Fearful of the unknown and influenced by media portrayals, my mind raced with worst-case scenarios. The thought of being taken to an undisclosed location triggered deep-seated anxieties, though thankfully, reality didn't align with those fears. Still, every passing minute felt like an eternity during that ride to the precinct. The heat bore down on me relentlessly, causing sweat to bead on my skin and my palms to grow clammy. Nervous energy coursed through me, setting my hands to shaking in a way I'd never experienced before. It was a feeling of uncharted territory, an unfamiliar blend of anticipation and apprehension. The processing at the facility was thorough, leaving no stone unturned. Stripped of personal items, subjected to meticulous searches, photographed, and fingerprinted, I navigated through the impersonal routine of intake procedures.

The loss of personal autonomy, even temporarily, was a reminder of the seriousness of the situation. As I reflect on my journey, I find myself confronting a difficult truth: the unresolved issues from my past are catching up to me. One of the most glaring examples of this is my decision to stop paying child support and instead send money directly to my daughter. While my intentions were undoubtedly good-hearted, the action itself was irresponsible. It's a sobering realization that even with the best intentions, our actions can have unintended consequences. Housed in a holding cell until my court appearance on Monday, the weekend loomed ahead with uncertainty. Each passing moment served as a reminder of the consequences of neglecting responsibilities, be it financial obligations or personal conduct. It was a weekend marked by introspection, regrets, and a determination to emerge from this ordeal with lessons learned and accountability taken. It was a profound lesson in humility, resilience, and the need for mindful decision-making in all aspects of life. After being confined to my cell for most of the day, I finally had the chance to make a phone call. Dialing my cousin's number, I relayed the harsh reality of my situation and my whereabouts. Engaging in conversation with him brought a sense of reproach, leaving me feeling exposed and isolated in a room bustling with unfamiliar faces, each with their own inscrutable agendas. It was a scenario I never imagined myself in — arrested and confined behind bars. The gravity of the situation began to dawn on me as they abruptly ended the phone call and instructed me to return to my cell, signaling the impending closure of our cell doors for the night. That first night in jail hit me like a ton of bricks. Tears flowed freely as I grappled with the consequences of my actions, feeling a deep sense of regret washing over me. Locked in that cell, I couldn't shake the feeling of losing my freedom in an instant. It was a sobering moment, forcing me to reflect on the choices that led me here and vow to make better ones in the future.

Alone in the darkness with a mind full of regrets and uncertainties, I found solace in prayer. There I was, on that hard, unforgiving bed, feeling the chill seep into my bones as I wrestled with my thoughts. The irony wasn't lost on me – once a celebrated athlete, now confined and battling current struggles and confinement. Each morning was a rude awakening, an eye-opening reminder of the grim reality I found myself in. Waking up with dry contact lenses stuck to my eyes, facing the day without even the basic amenities like soap for a decent shower, and having to contend with spoiled food—all within the confines of our unit, with no access to the outdoors. It was a daily struggle against both physical discomfort and the mental anguish of confinement. My cellmates, also in for child support issues, became companions in adversity as we whiled away hours playing cards and sharing stories as we got to know one another. The monotony of the days was broken only by the anticipation of Monday morning—the day we were set to face the judge and, hopefully, gain our freedom.

As Monday arrived, we were roused early and ushered into a makeshift courtroom within the jail, complete with cameras linking us to the actual courtroom where our families watched anxiously from the actual courtroom. Waiting my turn outside the courtroom, I observed the varying emotions of relief and hope among those exiting after their hearings. Facing the judge was like stepping onto a battlefield, except instead of weapons, harsh words were the ammunition. The judge's tone dripped with disdain, as if my efforts to support my daughter were nothing but empty gestures. She dismissed the money I sent directly to her mother as mere gifts, refusing to acknowledge their significance. Then came the crushing blow: I was ordered to pay a hefty $10,000 to secure my release. It felt like a cruel joke, a sum that seemed utterly unattainable given my dire financial circumstances.

The experience was a constant reminder of the stereotypes that often haunt professional athletes. Despite assumptions of wealth and prosperity, the reality was far from glamorous. I was barely scraping by, struggling to make ends meet like so many others in similar situations. Being judged through the lens of my past success on the field only added insult to injury, highlighting the vast chasm between perception and reality. Returning to the unit with the news, disbelief echoed among my fellow inmates, none of whom had encountered such a daunting release fee. As families began making payments for others and one by one, inmates left, I faced the harsh reality of being trapped without immediate recourse. My family rallied behind me, gathering funds and negotiating with authorities to secure my release. However, the process dragged on, each passing moment amplifying my desperation. When the wired funds weren't immediately available, I confronted the grim prospect of spending another day confined, a thought I couldn't bear.

Turning to my brother for assistance, he contacted my coach in Canada on my behalf, explaining the dire situation and my imminent absence from practices and meetings. Recognizing the urgency, my coach and team acted swiftly, arranging for the necessary funds to expedite my release. As my brother awaited the final transaction, the agonizing uncertainty of potential additional incarceration weighed heavily on me, making every passing second feel like an eternity. While in that confined space, reflections on life, choices, and faith flooded my mind. I couldn't help but ponder the path that had led me to that cell—how a series of decisions, some reckless and impulsive, had culminated in this moment of realization. The contrast between my former life of athletic prowess, public admiration, and financial stability to the present reality of incarceration and financial woes weighed heavily on my psyche.

The interactions with my fellow inmates, each with their own stories of adversity and struggle, provided a humbling perspective. In the Bible, Paul offers words of profound encouragement that many of us turn to during our most challenging times. In that moment of despair, his message resonated deeply with me: "I can do all things through Christ who strengthens me" (Philippians 4:13). This scripture, often quoted when we face seemingly insurmountable obstacles, provided a beacon of hope and strength for me in that trying time. What we fail to realize is what comes before those profound words from a man who was writing this from a prison cell. He stated "I know what it is to be in need, and I know what it is to have plenty. I have learned the secret of being content in any and every situation, whether well fed or hungry, whether living in plenty or in want. As seconds turned to minutes and minutes turned into hours, the resilience that had shaped my athletic career was now being tested in a completely different arena—one filled with personal trials and my struggle for redemption. Finally, the anticipated call came—a ray of hope piercing through the gloom of uncertainty. My brother's voice, tinged with relief and urgency, informed me of the imminent resolution. The wired funds had cleared, and arrangements for my release were in motion.

The thought of finally leaving that cramped cell and breathing the air of freedom again brought an overwhelming sense of relief and gratitude. When the guard called my name and opened the cell door, it felt surreal. Each step out of that confined space was a mix of disbelief and anticipation. I clutched my few belongings tightly, each one a small piece of my tumultuous journey. As I was processed out, the minutes felt like hours. The paperwork, the procedural formalities—all seemed to drag on, yet they were the final hurdles to reclaiming my liberty. The finality of hearing the cell door clang shut behind me for the last time was a sound I would never forget. Once outside, the air felt different—fresher, richer, more vibrant. It was like tasting freedom for the first time. I couldn't afford to waste a moment. I immediately headed to clear the hold on my passport, a bureaucratic tangle that had kept me anchored in this painful chapter of my life.

With the hold finally lifted, I wasted no time booking a flight back to Canada. The urgency was palpable. I needed to put distance between myself and the place that had held me captive, both physically and mentally. The process of booking the flight was almost mechanical; my mind was focused solely on getting back to familiar grounds, to the people and places that mattered most. The flight itself was a blur. I spent most of the time reflecting on the ordeal, the choices that led me here, and the path ahead. It was daunting to think about rebuilding, yet there was a sense of renewed purpose. I was no longer the same person who had entered that cell. The experience, as harrowing as it was, had reshaped my perspective on life and liberty.

Landing in Canada felt like crossing a finish line after a grueling race. The relief was immense, but so was the awareness of the challenges still to come. Yet, as I stepped onto Canadian soil, I was determined to approach these challenges with the same determination that had fueled my athletic career. This was a new chapter, a chance to reaffirm my resilience and rebuild my life with a deeper understanding of freedom and responsibility. As the year transitioned and I decided to remain in Canada during the offseason, it was a departure from the usual routine where players typically returned home to spend time with their families and unwind. This decision was made with the intent of exploring career opportunities, extending my contract, and immersing myself further into the Canadian football scene. Little did I know that this period would unfold into a journey filled with unforeseen challenges and profound personal growth.

Unlike previous off-season's where I had concrete plans or engagements to occupy my time, this was the first time I found myself in a void of uncertainty. Despite having avenues for employment in Canada and a path towards contract extension, a lingering sense of unease gnawed at me, urging me to confront unresolved issues and take ownership of my responsibilities that I left back home.

Change was sparked by an unexpected call from my kids' aunt in Texas. She revealed that the kids and their mother had returned to Texas, along with distressing news about their imminent eviction. This revelation shook me to the core, amplifying my feelings of guilt and obligation towards my kids. Without hesitation, I rose to the challenge. I informed my manager that I had a family emergency and regrettably had to turn down the job I had just accepted. My children needed me, and I needed to be there to provide relief and support. Reflecting on my past decisions, I realized I had abandoned my children in pursuit of a dream that had lost its passion and purpose. What once drove me had morphed into an unhealthy obsession and an escape from reality, a way to cling to something I was good at instead of facing my responsibilities. Now, it was time to prioritize what truly mattered and make amends for the time I had lost. I booked a flight back to Texas, determined to provide immediate assistance and secure a stable living situation for my children and their mother.

Upon arriving in Texas, I opted to stay in a hotel while embarking on a tireless search for suitable housing. The urgency of the situation fueled my determination, and after thorough exploration, I managed to secure a rental home—a temporary place as I navigated the storm of uncertainty in that season. Transitioning into this new phase brought a myriad of emotions. Reuniting with my children filled me with joy, yet the weight of the circumstances and strained interactions with their mother loomed heavily over me. These moments unveiled to me the palpable tension and underscored the need for decisive action and positive change. I stayed in the house and shared a room with my son. It was a strange and awkward situation, one that was confusing for them and led to many heartfelt conversations. Despite the challenges, there were moments of joy and fun. Being in the same home as my children allowed us to reconnect in ways I had missed while chasing my dreams. We laughed together, played games, and shared stories late into the night.

However, the underlying tension was always there, making it uneasy. I enjoyed the time with my kids, but I couldn't ignore the unhealthy environment I was living in. The uncertainty about the future weighed heavily on me, and I knew I needed to find a way to provide stability for them and for myself. It was a bittersweet time, balancing the happiness of being close to my children with the discomfort of living in a situation that was far from ideal. The pivotal family meeting I called served as a platform to express my love and commitment to my children while acknowledging the necessity of restructuring our living arrangements. The decision to move out, although challenging, stemmed from a deep-rooted desire to set a positive example and foster a healthier environment for everyone involved. With housing secured and family matters addressed, I turned my attention to securing stable employment to sustain myself and contribute towards my children needs. Landing a job as a delivery driver for a catering company provided a financial foothold, albeit modest, during these uncertain times.

However, fate had another twist in store with the onset of the Covid-19 pandemic. The abrupt disruption to daily life, coupled with economic uncertainties, cast a shadow of apprehension over my newfound stability. The first paycheck from my job, while a relief, quickly dwindled due to essential expenses and unforeseen deductions like child support taking more than 80%, leaving me financially strained. After talking with the kids and watching the news about the world going into lockdown, I still chose to step into the unknown, unaware of the seriousness of what was about to unfold. At first, it seemed like people were overreacting. Stores were closing early, shelves were being emptied as families stocked up on essentials, and everyone was hunkering down with their loved ones. Meanwhile, I found myself alone in an Airbnb, trying to navigate this new reality.

It was a surreal experience. The streets were eerily quiet, and the usual hustle and bustle of life had come to a standstill. I had stepped out in faith, determined to do the right thing, but the uncertainty was overwhelming. My decision to leave behind an unhealthy situation had thrust me into a new set of challenges. I was trying to figure out how to maintain and survive in this unprecedented time, far from the comfort and security of my family. The isolation was daunting, and the weight of my choices pressed heavily on me as I grappled with the fear and uncertainty of the world outside my temporary home. The realization that I had exhausted financial reserves brought from Canada for housing and initial expenses further compounded my challenges. As the pandemic-induced lockdown took hold, the prospect of surviving on a minimum-wage job in a foreign setting became daunting. The isolation from family and support networks added to the emotional toll of navigating through uncharted territory. Returning to Texas, while a necessary step to ensure my children's well-being, symbolized a bittersweet chapter marked by resilience and humility.

Each day became a testament to adaptability and perseverance, fueled by a deep-seated sense of responsibility and the unwavering determination to weather the storm. As we all sat at home, with the world seemingly on pause, the escalating racial tensions weighed heavily on my mind. The news was filled with stories of injustice and brutality, forcing me to reflect deeply on what it meant to be a Black man in America. It was bewildering and disheartening to see that, after all this time, police officers and others could still be so cruel and discriminatory.

These reflections weren't just theoretical—they permeated my everyday life. Each time I stepped out of my door, I was acutely aware of the potential dangers that could arise simply because of the color of my skin. The fear was not just for myself, but for my children and loved ones as well. The world outside felt increasingly hostile, and the pervasive sense of unsafety was hard to shake. This period of reflection was intense and all-consuming. The combination of a global pandemic and the reality of racial injustice left me feeling vulnerable and anxious. The enforced isolation provided ample time to ponder these issues, and it became clear that the fight for justice and equality was far from over. It was a sobering reminder of the long road ahead and the importance of continuing to advocate for change. Looking back on that chaotic stretch, now I can see the important lessons it brought me: about toughness, thinking on my feet, and the strength we carry within. Each trial, every setback, and all those tough choices—they all played a part in reshaping how I saw things and how I faced them. They helped me find a new drive, a fresh sense of purpose, steering me towards a future that feels brighter, one filled with hope and chances waiting to be seized.

It was the new normal, a phrase that seemed to encapsulate the strange, uncertain reality we were all living in. For the time being, I was grateful to have a roof over my head, clothes to wear, and food to eat. As I scrolled through social media, I couldn't help but notice how families were coming together, sharing stories, and posting about the creative and heartwarming activities they were doing with their loved ones. At the same time, I saw the devastating news of people losing their lives to the virus. Meanwhile, I was stuck in an Airbnb with a group of strangers. Each of us was confined to our own room, barely interacting except for brief encounters in the hallway. It felt eerily reminiscent of my freshman year in college, living in a dorm and being forced to share space with strangers. Back then, we made the best of it and eventually became close friends. This time, however, the sense of isolation was palpable, and the camaraderie of those dorm days felt like a distant memory. I reminded myself daily that things could be much worse, and I tried to hold onto that gratitude. But there was an underlying anxiety that never quite left me.

As my resources dwindled, the fear of returning to where I started loomed large. Living in an Airbnb, watching my savings steadily decrease, I couldn't help but feel a sense of impending doom. Each day brought a new challenge, and though I was managing to keep my head above water, the effort was exhausting. I was constantly calculating, trying to stretch every dollar and make every meal last a little longer. The uncertainty was relentless, gnawing at me as I lay awake at night, wondering how much longer I could keep this up. As the days stretched on, each one seeming longer than the last, I found myself constantly grappling with difficult choices. Every decision about how to use my limited resources felt like a high-stakes game of survival. Should I fill up my car with gas to get to work, or should I buy a meal to keep my energy up? In those moments, the dollar menu at fast food restaurants became my best friend, providing just enough sustenance to keep me going. The world outside was filled with tension and unrest, and inside, my own struggles were no less daunting. My initial sense of resilience began to waver. The isolation of the pandemic, combined with my precarious financial situation, created a pressure cooker of stress and fear.

I tried to maintain a positive outlook, focusing on the small victories—an unexpected refund, a kind word from a friend, a good day with my children. But beneath the surface, I was acutely aware that my resources were running out. The safety net I had cobbled together was fraying, and I was teetering on the edge of falling right back into the dire straits I had fought so hard to escape. Despite the dire circumstances, I knew I couldn't afford to give up. The thought of my children kept me pushing forward, looking for any opportunity to turn things around. I applied for jobs relentlessly, took on odd gigs, and even considered paths I had never thought I'd have to walk. The new normal was a test of endurance, resilience, and sheer willpower. It was a constant battle to keep going, to keep fighting for a better future. And though the days were often filled with doubt and worry, there was also a glimmer of hope that kept me moving forward, step by step, through the uncertainty and the fear.

CHAPTER 5: SUSPENDED

Temporarily banned the player from participating in games and related team activities due to a violation of league rules or policies.

Navigating the intricate paths of life's transitions often feels like traversing a dense forest blindfolded, uncertain of what lies ahead. One such pivotal juncture for me arose after taking time off from the NFL, experiencing the pangs of forced retirement, and then deciding to revisit my football roots in the CFL. However, amidst this professional turmoil, a seed of alternative pursuit sprouted in my mind—an interest in male physique bodybuilding. The allure of merging my passion for nutritional health with the rigors of weightlifting to sculpt my physique to new heights beckoned me. This wasn't just about physical transformation but also about channeling discipline and determination into a different arena. Venturing into this domain, I sought out supplements, cautious due to my prior adherence to strict regulations governing performance-enhancing substances in professional sports.

A testosterone booster from GNC marked my initial foray into this realm, and the immediate surge of energy and vigor it provided fueled my aspirations. However, what I hadn't fully anticipated were the lingering traces of these supplements in my system, a fact that would unravel upon my return to Canada and the resumption of professional testing protocols. The test results, weeks delayed but impactful nonetheless, carried the weight of consequence—a suspension from the team for two critical games due to elevated testosterone levels, a violation under the stringent substance use policy. This suspension wasn't just about missing games; it was a form of isolation within the team dynamic—a separation from practice sessions, team camaraderie, and crucial strategizing meetings. The sting of isolation intensified as I found myself on the receiving end of accusations, spoken to as though I was intentionally seeking an unfair advantage. It was as if every interaction was laced with suspicion and distrust, leaving me feeling misunderstood and unfairly judged. This period of exclusion paralleled the eerie isolation experienced during the Covid lockdowns. The desolate streets mirrored the void within, a lack of physical connections accentuating the solitude. The absence of routine team interactions resonated with the newfound silence of deserted roads and shuttered establishments.

With livelihood concerns looming large, I embarked on a multifaceted journey—a blend of academic pursuit and strategic survival decisions. Enrolling in life coaching studies marked a proactive step towards personal and professional growth. Amidst all the chaos, I kept my focus on completing my graduate degree, thanks to the NFL scholarship. It was a lifeline of sorts,

SUSPENDED

keeping me anchored through the storm. Despite the turmoil in other aspects of my life, advancing academically brought a sense of fulfillment and purpose that helped me stay on track. Yet, financial constraints necessitated unconventional solutions. I emptied my savings and found myself living out of my car, finding solace in the secluded corner of a park's parking lot each night. It was a makeshift haven, tucked away from prying eyes and offering a semblance of safety as I slept with my seat leaned back and my firearm next to me. This adjustment wasn't just about making it through each day, but also a testament to the strength and flexibility I found within myself when confronted with challenges.

In hindsight, these moments of isolation and adaptation weren't just about circumstantial challenges but profound lessons in resourcefulness, humility, and resilience. They were chapters of metamorphosis, shaping not just my physique but also my mindset, preparing me for the unpredictable terrain of life beyond the gridiron. Moving to a position with Amazon marked a significant shift from my previous role at the catering company. Recognizing the need for a more stable source of income, I took on this new challenge, understanding that it would require a lot from me. However, I saw it as a step in the right direction—a move towards sustainability at a time when the world seemed to stand still. After a few weeks, a significant transition occurred in my circumstances—a decisive move from the uncertainties of living in my car to the stability of residing in an Airbnb once again. This change not only improved my living conditions but also rekindled a sense of routine and purpose that I had deeply missed. Driving for Amazon was both fun and rewarding. There was a unique satisfaction in delivering packages, knowing I was bringing a bit of joy or relief to someone's day.

One of the unexpected highlights was the way many homeowners would leave snacks and drinks outside for us, along with sweet messages of thanks. It was such a small gesture, but it made a world of difference. In a time where I often felt isolated and unseen, these acts of kindness reminded me that I was appreciated. Seeing those thoughtful notes and treats waiting for me kept a smile on my face, providing a much-needed boost to my spirits. It was a simple yet profound reminder that even in challenging times, there is still kindness and humanity all around us. Drawing from my professional athlete background, I maintained a disciplined schedule, adhering to a rigorous routine that began at 3:30 am every morning. This early rise wasn't just about physical preparation; it encompassed moments of spiritual grounding through prayer, time for personal growth with reading and schoolwork, and physical fitness at the gym. The gym, with its doors opening at 5:00 am, became my sanctuary—offering not just physical rejuvenation but also mental fortitude for the challenges ahead. It provided me with a sanctuary where I could finally relax and find some peace. The sauna became my safe haven, enveloping me in a warm, comforting embrace as I prayed and cried there daily. The showers kept me clean, and lifting weights offered the therapy and self-care I desperately needed.

SUSPENDED

During my commute to work, I immersed myself in inspirational content, listening to sermons by renowned speakers like Mike Todd, Steve Furtick, TD Jakes, and even motivational talks by Steve Harvey.

These messages weren't just echoes of positivity but pillars of strength and resilience during trying times. Sharing these insights with a close friend became a daily ritual, a symbiotic exchange of hope and encouragement that fueled us both amidst life's storms. The power of positive words became profoundly transformative during my darkest moments. Words of affirmation from my friend, labeling me as one of the strongest individuals he knew, became anchors that held me steady during turbulent emotional tides. They were lifelines that prevented me from succumbing to despair or making rash decisions born of desperation. As I navigated the open highways and streets on my delivery routes, devoid of the usual traffic chaos, I marveled at the simplicity and impact of human kindness. Despite the strides made in my professional life and financial stability, the lack of a permanent residence remained a looming challenge. Somehow, word got out about my situation—how I was bouncing between living in my car and staying in Airbnb's. One of my friends, upon hearing this, reached out to me with genuine concern. He couldn't bear the thought of me enduring another day like that. Having recently bought a new home with a spare room, he insisted I come stay with him. His generosity and unwavering support were a lifeline, offering not just a roof over my head, but a sense of stability and belonging during a turbulent time.

His compassion and quick action not only provided a roof over my head but also reinstated a sense of camaraderie and support that I sorely needed. In these moments of transition and transformation, I learned invaluable lessons about resilience, humility, and the profound impact of genuine connections. Each step forward wasn't just about personal progress but also about embracing vulnerability and allowing others to uplift and support me—a humbling yet empowering realization that reshaped my outlook on life and relationships. Entering the house for the first time was a moment of profound relief and gratitude. The kindness shown to me by my friend as he guided me to my room evoked overwhelming emotions, causing me to drop to my knees in tears. His home was beautiful, a sanctuary that offered me the fresh start I desperately needed to get my life back in order. In that moment, I felt a profound sense of reassurance, a reminder that God had not forgotten about me amidst my struggles.

What I truly longed for was a sense of permanence and security. With this in mind, I decided to unpack the totes and organize their contents into closets and drawers. However, I found myself still living out of the garage, with the bulk of my clothes stored away. Determined to manifest my faith in securing my own place soon, I made plans to retrieve the rest of my belongings from Detroit and store them in a storage unit, anticipating a future with more stability and assurance. With the unwavering support of my cousin, we rented a U-Haul and embarked on an 18-hour journey back to Texas, a testament to the power of family bonds and the help we can give each other when times get tough. My cousin's consistent presence and willingness to lend a helping hand were invaluable. He not only helped me pack and transport my belongings but also unpacked everything upon our arrival in Texas. Despite his busy schedule, he ensured that I was settled before flying back to Detroit the following day. With my belongings finally in place, I felt a renewed sense of stability and hope for the future.

Having a stable job and a newfound sense of security in my living situation allowed me to focus on personal and professional development. As the world remained in lockdown, I maximized my time by applying for jobs, dedicating myself to spiritual growth through fasting, prayer, and daily sermons. As the lockdown unfolded, it started off with a lot of uncertainty hanging in the air. But surprisingly, as the days went by, I began to feel a sense of peace settle in. It was like the world hit the pause button, giving everyone—including me—a chance to catch their breath. For once, the relentless hustle and bustle of everyday life seemed to fade into the background. With everything on hold, I found myself with the time and space to catch up on things I'd put off and to reassess where I was headed. It was a relief to know I wasn't alone in navigating these challenging times. And with that newfound stability, I could finally focus on making strides towards my transition into the corporate world. No longer confined to the streets, I saw the opportunity to carve out a future beyond mere survival.

My manager caught wind of my name, did some research, and learned that I was a former NFL player. One day, he made a comment to me about why I was working there given my past success in football. His words stung, piercing through my fragile sense of self-worth. It was a harsh reminder of my fall from grace yet again, how I had gone from being a prominent football player to driving for Amazon and barely making ends meet. The contrast between my past glory and present struggle felt like a heavy weight, pressing down on me and highlighting the gap between where I had been and where I was now. It underscored the harsh reality of how quickly life can change, leaving me to grapple with the feeling of not living up to my potential and questioning my place in the world.

It was during this introspective period that I had a conversation on the phone with a friend and told him about my current situation and he introduced me to a program offered by the NFL for former players, emphasizing professional and personal development opportunities. Intrigued by the prospect, I pursued the opportunity and, after a rigorous interview process, secured a role in the six-month program. The program not only provided valuable experience and skill development but also allowed me to interact with fellow former NFL players navigating life beyond the game. Despite being in a similar transitional phase myself, the program offered clarity and direction, helping me chart a course for my post-football life. Reflecting on my journey, I acknowledged that I hadn't adequately planned for life after football—a realization that underscored the importance of seizing opportunities for growth and adaptation.

The difference between my public persona as a former NFL player and my current position was striking, bringing forth a blend of appreciation for the job and a tinge of embarrassment for not meeting the standards set by past accomplishments. However, this encounter served as a catalyst for change, igniting a determination to succeed in the corporate world with the same tenacity I had exhibited on the field. Upon receiving the offer, I found myself back at Amazon, ready to deliver the news to my manager. His unintentional comment had struck a chord within me, igniting a fire to aim higher and recognize my own worth beyond the confines of being a delivery driver. With gratitude, I expressed my appreciation for the opportunity, yet firmly conveyed my decision to move on. My manager, ever gracious, assured me of a warm welcome should I choose to return. However, I knew deep down that my path was leading elsewhere. This season had served its purpose, but it was time to ascend to greater heights. I left with the door open for future connections, acknowledging the value of the journey while embracing the new horizons ahead.

Opting to shift gears from Amazon to the NFL program marked a pivotal moment in my journey, signaling my determination to reclaim my ambitions and dreams. It was a conscious choice to embrace the belief that setbacks are not permanent roadblocks but rather opportunities for learning and transformation. This decision was both humbling and empowering. Working with the NFL was not just an opportunity but a transformative experience that opened doors to a wealth of resources and connections crucial for my journey forward. It was more than just fun; it was a platform that allowed me to delve into meaningful projects like developing newsletters, mental health counseling, job shadowing programs, and engaging sessions with best-selling authors. However, the true value lay in the weekly counseling sessions facilitated by remarkable counselors virtually, providing invaluable insights and support. The internship experience was enriched by the presence of an exceptional mentor who not only guided me professionally but also embodied qualities of a devoted father and husband. His mentorship was not just about equipping me with job skills but nurturing character traits and interpersonal skills crucial for success.

His investment in my development went beyond what was expected, and I am grateful for the wisdom and encouragement he shared. During one of our career fair events, a particular company piqued my interest with its mission and opportunities. Recognizing the transferable skills possessed by former players, they expressed immediate hiring needs. Seizing the moment, I reached out to them promptly, expressing my keen interest and intent to contribute to their team. Concurrently, the impending vacancy due to my mentor's departure for a full-time coaching role presented an intriguing opportunity within the NFL program. As the six-month internship drew to a close, I found myself at a crossroads, facing a pivotal decision. On one hand, there was the opportunity to transition into a full-time role within the company where I had been interning. It was a path familiar to me, offering stability and continuity. On the other hand, there was the allure of a new journey, presented through a job in the eye care field. Each option carried its own set of risks and rewards. Accepting the full-time role would provide a sense of security and familiarity, allowing me to build upon the foundation I had already established during my internship. However, it also meant committing to a known path, potentially limiting my exposure to new experiences and opportunities for growth.

On the contrary, embarking on the new journey presented a realm of possibilities. The eye care world offered a glimpse into a different industry or role, igniting my curiosity and sparking a desire for exploration while staying rooted in Texas. It was a chance to step out of my comfort zone, embrace uncertainty, and chart a course towards personal and professional development. Ultimately, the decision weighed heavily on my shoulders, as I carefully considered the implications of each choice. Yet, amidst the uncertainty, there was a sense of excitement and anticipation for the path that lay ahead. Whether I chose to embrace familiarity or venture into the unknown, I was confident that it would mark the beginning of a new chapter in my journey. As I navigated the interview processes for both opportunities, financial challenges weighed heavily on my mind. In a moment of humility and need, I turned to prayer, specifically asking for $1000, a sum I needed urgently but felt hesitant to request from anyone I knew. Putting aside my pride, a daunting task in itself, I reached out to a friend who did my taxes for help. When they inquired about the amount, I simply asked for whatever they could spare. Surprisingly, they sent over exactly $1000 through Cash App without me saying an amount. It was a timely answer to a prayer uttered in solitude, altering the course of that season for me and providing the boost I needed to move forward without falling behind.

The decision-making process regarding job offers was multifaceted, considering factors such as career growth, financial stability, and personal alignment. While the allure of staying in familiar territory in Texas was enticing, the prospect of contributing to player development and leveraging my NFL experience in New York held significant appeal. After prudent consideration and seeking God in prayer, I carefully thought through the opportunity in New York with confidence and conviction. Transitioning to New York would represent more than a career move; it would symbolize a commitment to impactful work and personal growth for people that had similar struggles like me. Despite the challenges of uprooting, the prospect of positively influencing lives and being part of an esteemed institution like the NFL resonated deeply. It was a decision not just about geographical relocation but about embracing a new chapter filled with purpose and possibilities. The journey from adversity to opportunity underscored the importance of resilience, faith, and seizing moments of grace.

SUSPENDED

Each step, from financial struggles to professional crossroads, reinforced valuable lessons in humility, determination, and gratitude. The allure of the NFL job was undeniable—a chance to remain connected to the world of professional sports, albeit from a different angle. However, upon careful reflection, I realized that it wasn't the right move for me. Instead of chasing the next big thing impulsively, I chose to stay in Texas and venture into the unfamiliar territory of eye care. It was a decision rooted in a desire to build lasting roots and to resist the temptation of jumping at opportunities without considering their long-term implications. Reflecting on my journey, I couldn't ignore the toll my pursuit of dreams, both healthy and unhealthy, had taken on my children and those around me. It dawned on me that I no longer wanted to live that life. Instead, I desired to be a present father, showing up consistently for my kids every single day. However, this wouldn't be feasible if I remained in New York while my children were in Texas. In the opening of this chapter, I delved into the sense of isolation I felt during the suspension I experienced. It felt like I was serving my time for past disobedience. However, as this season of my life progressed, I found myself given another chance. The opportunity to practice with the team again emerged, signaling a chance for redemption and preparation to get back in the game.

CHAPTER 6: TIMEOUT

A timeout refers to a brief pause in gameplay during which the clock is stopped and players and coaches can regroup, discuss strategies, make substitutions, or receive instructions from their coaches.

Reflecting on the journey that led me to this transformative phase in my life, I can't help but acknowledge the twists and turns that shaped my perspectives and choices. It's not merely a sequence of events but a narrative interwoven with moments of reckoning, introspection, and resilience. The echoes of Jesus' wisdom in Luke 14:28-30 resonate profoundly with my experiences. *'But don't begin until you count the cost. For who would begin construction of a building without first calculating the cost to see if there is enough money to finish it? 29Otherwise, you might complete only the foundation before running out of money, and then everyone would laugh at you. 30They would say, 'There's the person who started that building and couldn't afford to finish it!'*

I often navigated through life with a strong sense of determination but sometimes overlooked the broader implications of my decisions. My childhood dream of excelling in football fueled my ambition, but it also became a consuming force that sometimes clouded my judgment. In pursuing personal goals, I inadvertently caused ripples in the lives of those around me, a truth that became increasingly evident during the maturation process. Returning to football after a hiatus marked a significant chapter. It wasn't merely about the game; it represented a quest for purpose and identity. However, as the curtain fell on my football career in Saskatchewan, I confronted a poignant reality. It was time to reconcile with past missteps and prioritize aspects of life that truly mattered, notably being a devoted father and a responsible individual guided by moral integrity. Amidst career crossroads involving enticing offers from the NFL as the programs' Professional and Personal Development coach and Alcon as an eyecare sales rep, I embarked on a journey of deeper introspection. No longer solely fueled by personal ambition or the NFL brand, I found myself in search of a deeper purpose and identity. It was a journey guided by divine wisdom and spiritual discernment. The decision to stay rooted in Texas, close to my children, was more than a career move; it signified a profound shift in priorities, embracing familial bonds over professional pursuits as I began the maturation process.

Choosing to forgo a tempting opportunity to prioritize family connections stirred up a mix of reactions, revealing society's contrasting views on success and fulfillment. For me, it wasn't about following the typical path, but rather about aligning my decisions with my deepest values—a realization that brought profound clarity and inner peace. Transitioning into a new phase involved not just physical relocation but a psychological and spiritual realignment. Securing a place of my own symbolized reclaiming autonomy and responsibility, moving beyond dependency towards self-sufficiency and growth. This newfound independence mirrored my internal journey towards greater self-awareness and emotional maturity. A significant turning point in this phase was a profound spiritual renewal, culminating in a recommitment to my faith through baptism. Shedding past burdens and embracing a renewed sense of purpose brought unparalleled clarity and emotional liberation. This inner transformation rippled outward, influencing my interactions, decisions, and priorities.

Each step in this journey—from moments of vulnerability and introspection to decisive actions guided by faith—has contributed to a narrative of growth and resilience. Embracing life's challenges as catalysts for personal evolution, I've come to appreciate the intricate balance between ambition and humility, success and fulfillment. This ongoing journey is not just about reaching destinations but cherishing the lessons, relationships, and values that illuminate the path forward. During the following weeks, amidst the ups and downs of apartment hunting, a realtor I was collaborating with finally found me a place. Admittedly, it wasn't the most ideal apartment, but the landlord was understanding of my low credit score. However, this understanding came with a caveat—I had to make an additional payment as a safety net in case of any payment lapses.

TIMEOUT

Navigating the challenges posed by my credit score wasn't new territory for me. I faced countless rejections from apartment applications and struggled to even open a bank account. Ironically, this period coincided with my birthday month, which I decided to celebrate with a reflective trip to Mexico. The change of scenery allowed me to introspect deeply on my life's journey—tracing the challenging paths I had traversed and contemplating the promising roads God had laid out before me.

While in Mexico, I had the unique experience of graduating online, a fitting juxtaposition of modern challenges and achievements against the backdrop of Covid-19 restrictions. Sitting by the poolside, receiving my master's degree virtually, felt like a significant milestone. However, it also carried a tinge of melancholy, as I longed for the traditional joy of celebrating such accomplishments with loved ones. The prospect of an in-person graduation slated for September added to my anticipation, eagerly awaiting the chance to share this achievement with family and friends. Reflecting on my recent struggles, especially the financial turmoil that stemmed from past missteps, I acknowledged the considerable damage done to my credit score. This setback reverberated through various aspects of my life, from apartment rejections to difficulties in opening bank accounts. I resorted to unconventional methods such as cashing checks at Walmart and relying on reloadable cards—a testament to the lengths I went to manage my finances during that trying time.

However, perseverance coupled with timely opportunities brought about a shift. After diligently paying off debts and improving my financial standing, I made another attempt at opening a bank account. To my relief and surprise, my application was accepted, signifying a turning point in my financial rehabilitation. It was a small victory, but it marked the beginning of a gradual upturn in my circumstances. The pivotal internship opportunity provided by the NFL was a beacon of hope during this period of transition. Collaborations with companies like Alcon not only broadened my professional horizons but also showcased new pathways for former athletes. Through these partnerships, I discovered unforeseen career avenues, including roles in the eye care industry. The irony wasn't lost on me—having once relied on contact lenses to pursue my athletic dreams, I now found myself potentially contributing to others' eye care journeys.

A significant influence during this time was another mentor, whose mentorship played a crucial role in my professional growth. His expertise as a personal trainer transcended fitness; he imparted valuable lessons in navigating corporate life and striving for success. Despite the challenges posed by closed buildings and remote work setups, the flexibility afforded by my new role allowed me to strike a balance between work commitments and cherished family moments.

The journey from financial instability to professional growth and renewed personal insights underscored the adage of perseverance amidst adversity. Each obstacle became a steppingstone, guiding me towards a more resilient and purpose-driven phase in life. These experiences not only shaped my career trajectory but also instilled a deeper appreciation for the interconnectedness of life's challenges and blessings. Reflecting on the journey from that pivotal conversation in the sauna in the first chapter, to the twists and turns that led me to a transformative month, I find myself in awe of life's complexities. May holds a blend of emotions for me—joy intertwined with grief; celebration mingled with sorrow. It marks the anniversary of my birth and the birth of my son, yet it also carries the weight of loss—the passing of a beloved friend from childhood and the sudden departure of my father. Amidst these moments of profound significance, I experienced both a baptism and a heartfelt exchange with my father, where he uttered the words "I love you" for the first time as an adult. Sharing these experiences with the man in the sauna, I sought to convey the reality of our human struggles while affirming the enduring hope found in faith. As believers, we cling to the assurance that even in our darkest moments, God remains steadfast, guiding us through the storms and promising a future filled with blessings.

Embarking on my new job came with unexpected blessings, one of which was an in-person training session that brought all new hires to Texas. We were accommodated in Fort Worth, creating an ideal opportunity to bond outside the corporate setting. Having established connections with other former players through virtual meetings and chats, meeting them in person felt like reuniting with teammates from a past life. The camaraderie and team spirit we rekindled were reminiscent of our playing days, fostering a sense of belonging and shared experiences as if we were back in the locker room.

During our time together, one of the guys managed to secure tickets to a boxing event held at the Cowboys facility, which added an exciting twist to our training trip. Amidst the traffic en route to the venue, our conversations delved into deeper territories—our past struggles and the transformative journeys that brought us to this juncture. I found myself sharing candidly about the challenges I had faced and the profound changes I was experiencing as we connected. The authenticity of our dialogue paved the way for meaningful reflections on faith, personal growth, and the role of divine intervention in our lives. In those candid moments, I opened up about my renewed commitment to my faith journey. I spoke about the pivotal role of trusting in God wholeheartedly, citing teachings from Pastor Mike Todd regarding the significance of tithing and surrendering my heart to God completely.

My colleagues were moved by my testimony and the palpable transformation they witnessed, resonating with the shared desire for spiritual and material blessings. The following day, serendipity seemed to be at play again as we connected with new acquaintances through a colleague's friends living in the area. Over dinner, conversations naturally gravitated towards faith, and I felt an instant connection with one of the guests who shared profound insights from scripture. Discovering that he was part of the praise team at a local church I admired from afar further intrigued me. Invited to attend the church service where he would be singing, we eagerly accepted, despite a minor delay caused by oversleeping. As we walked into the packed service, the seating arrangement seemed almost providential—the last available seats were in the front row. Little did I know that this seemingly mundane decision would lead to an unexpected revelation. As the worship began, I was captivated by the angelic voice of a woman on stage—a presence that seemed to radiate light and grace. It was a moment of divine clarity; I felt an inexplicable connection that transcended mere coincidence. Sharing a glance with my friend, I knew he understood the significance of that moment in my quest for companionship and fulfillment in life that we discussed the night before.

The sermon that day centered around tithing, echoing the discussions we had been having about faith and divine alignment. It felt like a subtle confirmation from above, affirming the path I was on and the hopes I held dear. Despite my eagerness to connect with her after the service, she seemed to have disappeared amidst the crowd, leaving me with a mix of anticipation and uncertainty. Undeterred, I returned to the church the following week, driven by a desire not just for spiritual nourishment but also to unravel this intriguing connection I drove 45-minutes for. Sitting in the front row once again, my eyes scanned the stage expectantly, only to find a different lineup on the stage. Though she wasn't there, the warmth of the congregation and the uplifting atmosphere reassured me that I was in the right place. The journey, filled with serendipitous encounters and moments of divine guidance, became a testament to the intricate dance between faith, perseverance, and destiny. Each step forward was laden with purpose, and though the quest for companionship remained unresolved, the journey itself was a transformative experience—one that deepened my faith, enriched my connections, and illuminated the profound ways God orchestrates our paths.

CHAPTER 7: VICTORY

The kneel down is often called a "victory formation", as it is most often run by a winning team late in the game in order to preserve a victory.

As I eased into my nightly rituals, getting ready to dive into an online sermon to take my mind off the hunger pangs, I felt like I was standing on the edge of something big—a journey that blended my quest for spiritual growth with the blossoming of a new connection. It was one of those moments where you sense that things are about to change, and you can't help but feel excited about what lies ahead. The act of fasting and prayer during this time was not merely a physical discipline but a soulful endeavor, shedding distractions to focus on deeper spiritual contemplation. In this state of heightened awareness, I watched praise and worship sessions, allowing the melodies and messages to permeate my being, culminating in a heartfelt prayer before retiring for the night. The subtle yet profound reassurance I felt, though not in audible words, echoed through my spirit, affirming the path I was embarking upon. With a blend of trepidation and anticipation, I sought out avenues to connect with this intriguing lady from church, navigating the modern landscape of social media and digital communication.

    Reaching out to a mutual acquaintance I had met over dinner while in training, I confided in him about my experience and expressed my interest in connecting with someone he sung with. Through his assistance, I gained access to her social media profile. Delving into her online presence wasn't mere curiosity; it was a quest for understanding, compatibility, and shared values. Despite my initial reservations about where I stood in life, especially compared to her seemingly perfect and accomplished persona portrayed on social media, I couldn't shake the feeling of being unworthy of such a remarkable woman. Her highlight reel painted a picture of someone who had life figured out, with success and happiness at every turn. In contrast, I felt like I was still figuring things out and navigating my own challenges. It was daunting to consider the idea of pursuing someone who appeared to have it all together when I felt like I was still a work in progress.

    After spending considerable time reflecting on my own journey, bolstering my self-confidence, and reaffirming my understanding of who I am and what I stand for, I reached a pivotal moment of decision. Despite my initial apprehensions, I resolved that if this remarkable woman could see beyond the surface and glimpse the sincerity of my heart, there might be a chance for connection. With a sense of permission sought in prayer, I mustered the courage to send her a message, reminding myself that rejection or non-response were outcomes I could handle. This inner dialogue became a source of comfort, reassuring me that regardless of the outcome, my journey of self-discovery and growth would continue, leading me toward someone who would appreciate me for who I am. As I hit send on that message, I couldn't help but feel a rush of nerves mixed with hope. The waiting game began, each passing moment ratcheting up my anticipation. Finally, her response arrived, and I delved into conversation with a mix of excitement and caution. I made sure to tread carefully, respecting her boundaries by asking about her relationship status. To my delight, she revealed that she was single, opening the door for us to connect on a deeper level.

As our chat evolved from simple texts to heartfelt voice memos, it felt like we were peeling back layers of ourselves, revealing our true selves in a digital world. The decision to take our connection offline and meet in person was nerve-wracking yet exhilarating, a mix of anticipation and uncertainty. We agreed to rendezvous at a quaint coffee shop, eager to see if the chemistry we felt online would translate to real life. Arriving early, I navigated a whirlwind of emotions—anticipation, nervousness, and a resolve to be authentically myself, flaws and all. As we sat across from each other, the conversation delved deeper than small talk. I found myself opening up about the ups and downs of my journey—sharing the struggles and victories that had molded me into who I am today. She listened attentively, her own life appearing organized and put together in contrast to my tumultuous path. It was a raw and honest exchange, where I spoke of co-parenting challenges, past missteps, and the quest for redemption that had defined my existence.

Her response, marked by kindness and understanding, transcended societal judgments or superficial impressions. Instead, our conversation went beyond the surface—it tapped into the core of human connection. We found acceptance and empathy in each other's stories, realizing that we were both on a journey of growth and self-discovery. The hours spent talking weren't mere dialogue but a dance of souls, finding resonance amidst life's unpredictable melodies. In retrospect, that coffee shop meeting wasn't just a date but a convergence of past experiences, present hopes, and future possibilities. It symbolized the courage to embrace vulnerability, the beauty of acceptance, and the transformative power of genuine connections rooted in faith and authenticity. Our connection grew stronger as we lost track of time in that quaint coffee shop, the hours slipping away until closing time softly nudged us back to reality. We strolled around the corner, finding solace in each other's company, and extended our conversation over another round of drinks, relishing in the joy of intellectual exchange. It was a refreshing experience, engaging with someone who not only shared my penchant for thoughtful discussions but also articulated their ideas with clarity and depth.

VICTORY

As the night dwindled and the call of responsibilities grew louder, I reluctantly acknowledged the need to say goodbye. With an early morning flight looming on the horizon, I savored every moment of our interaction but knew I had to head home. Still buzzing with the excitement of our meeting, I confided in my brother, sharing the profound connection I felt and my unwavering belief that she was destined to be my life partner. This declaration of certainty wasn't just wishful thinking; it was a testament to the connection we shared on that fateful night. While I was back home in Detroit, reconnecting with my daughters and trying to make up for lost time, thoughts of having a life partner who accepted me completely lingered in my mind, overshadowing any problems that arose. When I wasn't catching up with my brother or spending time with my little ones, we would spend hours on FaceTime, chatting away. Even when the conversation ran dry, just being in each other's virtual presence was enough. I'm sure you can relate to those feelings when you first meet someone special, and the excitement is palpable.

It was during this time that I found myself not just sharing life updates but envisioning a future where we walked hand in hand. The upcoming milestone of my graduation in person loomed large, and I initially resigned myself to celebrating solo due to the unavailability of family and friends. This was a pivotal moment for me as I pursued my Master's degree. With everyone caught up in their own busy lives, I found myself navigating this journey alone, but it wasn't anything new for me. I've grown accustomed to handling things on my own for a while now, so while it may have felt lonely at times, I was determined to push through and achieve my goals. However, her unwavering support shattered my solo plans. She insisted on joining me, emphasizing the importance of shared moments and mutual encouragement. Her gesture went beyond mere companionship; it symbolized the beginning of a journey where we championed each other's successes. In the early stages of our relationship, she emphasized the significance of moments, reminding me that they're fleeting and irreplaceable. Her decision to come and support me during this milestone, despite our budding relationship, spoke volumes about her character and compassion. It warmed my heart and reassured me that she was the answer to my prayers.

Her presence at my graduation, unexpected yet profoundly meaningful, marked a turning point in our budding relationship. Amidst applause and accolades, her unwavering support stood as a testament to her character and the depth of our connection. Her thoughtful gesture extended beyond the stage as she surprised me with a celebratory dinner, the backdrop of the night painting a picture of shared dreams and mutual admiration. The setting was picturesque, the ambiance of the restaurant was enchanting, and the food was exquisite. But what truly touched me was her demeanor—she prayed over our meal, showered me with kindness, and treated me with a level of care and respect that felt unfamiliar yet deeply comforting. It was as if she had known me for years, anticipating my needs and desires before I even voiced them. As emotions welled up and tears streamed down my face, I felt a sense of restoration wash over me. In her presence, my broken heart found solace, and all the trials I had endured seemed to fade into the background. She saw me, celebrated me, and for that, I was immensely grateful.

As our relationship blossomed, serendipitous revelations unfolded, weaving a tapestry of divine alignment. It was revealed that on the day she responded to my Instagram message, she was engaged in a spiritual endeavor—a water fast accompanied by fervent prayers for a life partner. The synchronicity of our actions and intentions showcased a higher orchestration, a cosmic dance of two souls converging at the right moment just the way our heavenly father drew it up. Our shared stories, once disclosed, unveiled layers of providence guiding our paths toward each other. What began as an Instagram inquiry and a leap of faith blossomed into a beautiful connection nurtured by shared values, mutual respect, and unwavering faith. Our journey felt like destiny unfolding before us, woven with unexpected meetings and conversations that touched the depths of our souls. It was as if the universe conspired to bring us together, reminding us that some connections are destined to happen. Each moment shared, each word exchanged, seemed to affirm that we were meant to cross paths and walk this path together. It was a profound realization, reaffirming the belief that certain encounters are more than mere coincidence—they are divine appointments that shape our lives in ways we could never imagine.

Over the course of ten months, our relationship blossomed into a beautiful tapestry woven with shared experiences, heartfelt conversations, and mutual respect. I won't sugarcoat it—the road we traveled together wasn't always smooth sailing. It felt more like a rollercoaster ride, full of exhilarating highs and heart-wrenching lows, with unexpected twists and turns at every corner. We both carried the weight of past hurts and traumas, and there were moments when our conversations delved into uncomfortable territory. But amidst the challenges, we glimpsed the essence of who we truly were—the depth of our love for each other and our shared faith in Christ. We discovered a profound sense of compatibility and purpose in each other's lives, anchoring us through the storms and uncertainties. Our journey wasn't easy, but it was worth every bump in the road as it led us closer to one another and to God's plan for our lives. Watching her interact with my children, it was clear that she put in genuine effort to connect with them. She approached them with kindness and patience, earning their affection and trust over time.

As a father, seeing this connection blossom even when progress seems minimal, was incredibly important to me—it showed me that she was willing to invest in our family and be a positive influence in my children's lives. Her efforts were not unnoticed, and I appreciated her willingness to build meaningful relationships with my kids. Her kindness, thoughtfulness, and genuine acceptance of my family dynamics reinforced my belief that she was not only the right person for me but also a remarkable fit for our future blended family. The pivotal moment arrived when I decided to propose to her, a decision that carried the weight of a lifetime commitment. Preparing for this special day was nerve-wracking yet filled with excitement and anticipation. I wanted every detail to be perfect, so I made sure to involve her loved ones, organize "marry me" signs, balloons, and restaurant reservations. Ensuring her hair and nails were done, and arranging for a photographer added to the pressure, but I was determined to make it unforgettable. Despite my usual penchant for extravagance, I wanted this proposal to be a surprise, a moment she would cherish forever. The effort and planning were all worth it when I saw the joy and surprise on her face.

As I knelt in the gondola boat, my heart pounded with a mixture of nervous anticipation and profound certainty. The victory formation in football came to mind, symbolizing a strategic move to secure the win. Similarly, in my journey, this proposal marked a significant milestone toward a future filled with shared dreams and unwavering devotion. The essence of victory resonates deeply with my faith journey as well. Drawing inspiration from 1 John 5:4-5 *"For whatever is born of God overcomes the world; and this is the victory that has overcome the world—our faith. Who is the one who overcomes the world, but he who believes that Jesus is the Son of God?"*, I reflected on the power of faith in overcoming life's challenges. The parallels between football strategies and spiritual principles became apparent as I embraced the idea of running the clock out to secure victory, not just on the field but also in life's myriad battles. It was a resounding "Yes"! The dinner was fantastic, and seeing her delight in the surprise and the love and support from our families and friends was priceless. We set our sights on a destination wedding in Hawaii, surrounded by those closest to us. In the year leading up to it, anticipation mounted as we planned and dreamed about our special day.

Standing before the bluest waters and breathtaking mountains, exchanging vows felt surreal, like a dream we never wanted to wake up from. The reception overflowed with love and connection, and as the night drew to a close, a display of fireworks lit up the sky, fulfilling a childhood dream of mine. It was pure magic, a moment frozen in time that we'll always treasure. Together, we embraced new beginnings, including purchasing our first home and eagerly awaiting the arrival of our first child on June 14, 2024. These milestones are not just personal victories but also testaments to God's grace and guidance in our lives. So, what's next? With my wife's encouragement and belief, I am embarking on a transformative journey to reignite my passion for becoming a clinician. Witnessing societal challenges, especially among marginalized communities, fueled my determination to make a positive impact. Returning to school with the NFL's support, I am pursuing my master's degree in clinical Mental Health Counseling, merging my athletic discipline with a compassionate approach to help others heal.

VICTORY

Reflecting on this transformative journey, I am reminded of the power of alignment with God's will. Through prayer and trust, doors opened, leading to fruitful opportunities and protected paths. Every challenge, setback, and triumph contributed to shaping a narrative of growth, resilience, and unwavering faith. As I share these reflections in my book, I hope to inspire others to embrace their unique journeys with courage and faith. Just as every chapter in my life held significance, so does every moment in yours. Embrace challenges as opportunities, uncertainties as adventures, and setbacks as steppingstones to greatness. Your story is a testament to resilience, hope, and the boundless possibilities that await. Keep moving forward with passion, purpose, and unwavering faith, knowing that your best chapters are yet to be written. We eagerly await the inspiring stories that will emerge from your journey! Your story and your life do matter. Your testimony, the way you live and the experiences you've overcome, hold tremendous power. In the face of challenges, remember the strength found in the blood of the Lamb and in your own testimony. Fearlessness, born from a deep sense of purpose, can guide you through even the darkest of times. Revelation 12:11 *"And they have defeated him by the blood of the Lamb and by their testimony. And they did not love their lives so much that they were afraid to die."*

Much Love,

Thiggy

Salvation Prayer

If you're ready to give your life to Christ and be a part of the winning team, it's as simple as repeating and believing this prayer. Caution! It doesn't make your life easier, but it does give you an advocate to navigate the hard and dark times and you will never be alone.

Heavenly Father, I repent of my sins and surrender my life to you. I believe that Jesus Christ is the Son of God, that he died on the cross for my sins and rose on the third day for my Victory. I believe with my heart and confess with my mouth that Jesus is my Lord and Savior. Cleanse me, Renew me, Transform me, I'm YOURS, in Jesus' name, AMEN!

Welcome to the family!!

Romans 10:9-10 *"If you openly declare that Jesus is Lord and believe in your heart that God raised him from the dead, you will be saved. For it is by believing in your heart that you are made right with God, and it is by openly declaring your faith that you are saved."*

www.ingramcontent.com/pod-product-compliance
Lightning Source LLC
Chambersburg PA
CBHW051702160426
43209CB00004B/995